His Church
His Way

His Church His Way

Repairing Cracks In The Foundation

David Kalamen

© 2024 His Church His Way
Repairing Cracks In The Foundation
David Kalamen
ISBN 10: 1-988226-70-8
ISBN 13: 978-1-988226-70-5

All rights reserved.

Note: Scriptural quotes are from the Amplified Bible throughout, unless otherwise noted.

Published by

First Page Publishing
Peachland, B.C. Canada

Contents

Preface..	VI
Chapter 1: My Journey into the Apostolic	1
Chapter 2: Building His Church, His Way	5
Chapter 3: The Until Factor.......................	12
Chapter 4: The Ekklesia.............................	19
Chapter 5: The Spirit and the Word Speaking Together..	29
Chapter 6: Reconciling Today's Church to the Ekklesia...	37
Chapter 7: The Apostolic Fathering Movement...	40
Chapter 8: The Government of the Godhead..	47
Chapter 9: Seven Essential Values Impacting Governance in the Godhead...	52
Chapter 10: Placing Ourselves in Remembrance...	72
Chapter 11: A Church Model Built Upon the Values of the Godhead........................	85
Chapter 12: Repairing Foundational Cracks in Present Church Governance.....	102
Chapter 13: The Necessity and Joy in Transition...	134
About The Author......................................	143

Preface

I am a pastor's kid, born in 1952 in Campbellton, New Brunswick, Canada. While growing up, I saw the 'good, bad and ugly' of church function and government. I lived on top of or beside the church and listened through the air vents. What I saw and heard significantly impacted my life. Though I could not reject the existence of God, as God had demonstrated His supernatural power on numerous occasions, I grew up with great suspicions regarding the integrity and efficacy of the Church.

When God called me into ministry, I reluctantly yielded and went to Bible College. I loved God but did not love His Church as an institution, and often wondered why His grace had chosen me. That religious paradigm helped set the course for my life.

Years before planting Kelowna Christian Center, my life was on a dedicated journey to understand the nature, life, function and government of His Church. I studied every church governmental model and evaluated their strengths and weaknesses.

I had the privilege of participating in the Jesus Movement, engaging in the Charismatic Movement, and celebrating the Apostolic Movement, listening to what "the Spirit was saying to the Church" (Rev 3:6). My soul, as a leader, longed for simplicity, relevance and authenticity. However, it wasn't until the dawning of the Apostolic Movement that I saw what His Church could look like and I initiated and integrated what the Lord was saying to me into church practice. The dream of a new church model started there.

I have had the unique privilege and honour to serve alongside some incredible leaders over the past fifty years of ministry. However, the last forty-two years have been dedicated to growing Kelowna Christian Center's governance model as an apostolic team. Together, we were able to build a trans-generational staff of leaders who grew the vision with the same kind of passion. They were committed to spiritual fathering, trained in the same spiritual DNA, values and structure, and the Lord blessed us immensely, enlarging our spiritual inheritance and sphere of influence.

Between my father (Arnold), my son (Brodie) and I, the Kalamen family has modelled a trans-generational anointing and commitment and invested well over one hundred years shepherding the City of Kelowna.

Kelowna Christian Center Society, its leadership, ministry, operational, missional and educational teams continue to build on that calling and remain dedicated to fulfilling our City, Province, national and global commitments. We have tested the principles and values shared in this booklet and have seen the blessing of the Lord.

If the story of my journey is a source of help to you, I am grateful. If what I was taught can be caught through reading this, I will be thankful. I pray "that the God of our Lord Jesus Christ, the Father of glory, may grant you a spirit of wisdom and of revelation [that gives you a deep and personal and intimate insight] into the true knowledge of Him [for we know the Father through the Son]" (Eph 1:17).

Chapter 1
My Journey Into The Apostolic

"Learn to trust the journey, even when you don't understand it."
Lolly Daskal

"Never be afraid to trust an unknown future to a known God."
Corrie Ten Boom

My family has a long, rich history and heritage within the Pentecostal movement in Canada. I graduated from two schools: Western Pentecostal Bible College (now Summit Pacific College), and Southern California College (now Vanguard University). I was taught the more traditional implications of a denomination on the local church at Western, but I was introduced to the spontaneous, free-flowing function of street churches amid the Jesus Movement outpouring in California.

My initial calling to ministry occurred at a youth rally in Kamloops, British Columbia, where

God spoke to me: *"David, I am calling you to be a teacher. Go to Bible School."* I obeyed, and the calling to teach grew under a mandate to **"always be ready to give an answer to every man that asks you a reason of the hope that is in you"** (1 Pet 3:15, KJV). I say *'grew'* because one may be called, but until one acts on the call, it is not released.

The call to plant a new church, Kelowna Christian Center, created a challenge for me. I realized that I could not stay and function within my denomination. God had been speaking to me about church governance, and what God was saying did not align itself to their understanding of scripture. The decision to leave was not out of reaction to a person or a system. I sincerely believe it was a response to the leading of the Holy Spirit and to a revelation of His Word.

My second calling occurred in 1992 at an apostolic conference in Dallas, Texas, at the Convention Center. I attended it with my brother-in-law, Doug Schneider, as his heart was desirous of hearing a word from the Lord. During one of the sessions he threw his books on to my lap, ran to the altar, and received the *"laying on of hands"* from some Argentinian apostles.

When he came back to his seat, I asked him what happened. He said, *"I got it. I don't know what*

I got, but I got it." My response was, *"Wonderful! Now you hold my books."* Just then the session ended. I stood and asked the Lord for a new commission, just as Dr. Michael Brown from Pensacola was closing the session in prayer. In mid prayer he stopped and said, *"Romans 1:5-6,"* and continued to finish his prayer.

I immediately looked it up, as it resonated in my spirit, and it read: **"It is through Him that we have received grace and [our] apostleship to promote obedience to the faith and make disciples for His name's sake among all the Gentiles, and you also are among those who are called of Jesus Christ to belong to Him."**

I knew that I had to receive this *grace of apostleship* for it to manifest. That day was the beginning of an accelerated ministry trajectory that continues to touch many nations through a missional, transformational, and educational anointing.

Kelowna Christian Center Society's impact continues to grow in fulfillment of this Biblical mandate. It has become clear to me that when an apostolic gifting is responded to by a leader, the tide that lifts his boat in harbor lifts those around him. I am grateful that what began in my heart that day continues to grow in influence through spiritual sons and daughters who are carrying the apostolic calling in their hearts.

You will find that I refer to fathering throughout this manuscript. Please do not take it as a statement against women in leadership, or that mothering cannot occur. This is not a gender debate, but a concept of training involving investing in next generational leaders. Whether you are a male or female leader within His ekklesia, the principles and values I outline will be beneficial to your leadership and governance outcomes.

Chapter 2
Building His Church, His Way

"He was waiting expectantly and confidently, looking forward to the city which has fixed and firm foundations, whose Architect and Builder is God."
Hebrews 11:10

All of us understand that we are living in a transitional generation – between yesterday and tomorrow, what was, what is and what is to come. Christian sociologists are saying that this may be the generation that changes *the face of Christianity*. Many of us have been crying for just this sort of thing. We have known for a while that the modern-day church, its pulpit and pew, have been in trouble. We need to have the courage to fix what's broken.

What God is looking for are leaders who are willing to look at themselves and the churches God has given them stewardship over. Change must happen to leaders first before it can be transmitted to the church. Often, we as leaders must go through a *break down* before God can *break into* our lives and ministries. Then God can *break through* to our hearts, and through us, *break out* to the world in a dynamic new way. He must do something *to* us so He can do something *in* us before He can do something *through* us.

Transitional leaders are going to require wisdom from God to know how to delicately handle the new order of church without losing the essential goodness of the old order, and respecting the old paths while searching for the new paths of the Spirit to walk in.

However, with the writer of Deuteronomy, I say **"we have circled these mountains long enough"** (2:3). Like the new generation of Israelites entering Canaan, the Church must be willing to face giants our forefathers were not prepared to face. This may not be easy but it is vital for the health of His Church, His leaders, His people, and ultimately, the world.

There is an ache in every heart for a different kind of Church and a different kind of relational experience. We are looking for a cause, but it is more than that. We are looking for a cause that is worth living and dying for. Abraham was not settled, and neither are we.

We are looking for a *"kingdom that is firm and stable and cannot be shaken..."* (Heb 12:28). We are looking for a kingdom experience that expresses the character and the power of God and sees His Kingdom come to earth (Lu 11:2).

In Matthew 16:18, Jesus said to His disciples, **"I will build My Church; and the gates of Hades will not prevail against it"** (KJV). A few points of clarity and priority are important here. Jesus said…

1. *He* would build His Church: i.e. our job is to build what He is building the way He wants it built, opening the door to opportunity and blessing;
2. It is *His Church*: i.e. not ours, not the church of our choice, not owned by a leader, congregation or denomination, but built to glorify His Name;
3. *Hell would try to undermine* what He builds: i.e. there would be a spiritual battle to successfully build, remain and endure; and,
4. *Hell would not prevail*: i.e. the Church built His way would successfully stand under assault.

The Bible says regarding salvation, **"Whatsoever is born of God overcomes the world…"** (1 Jn 5:4, KJV). By comparison we could say, whatever is not born of God will *not prevail* against the world or religious systems. To apply that to the Church, it would be appropriate to say: *"whatever is built by God overcomes"* but *"whatever is man-made will be overcome."*

Anything God builds is built to last. Paul refers to His kingdom as an unshakable one. Listen to what Paul says about God's intention regarding His Church and kingdom in Hebrews 12:27-29 (Msg):

> ***"His voice that time shook the earth to its foundations; this time—he's told us this quite plainly—he'll also rock the heavens: One last shaking, from top to bottom, stem to stern." The phrase "one last shaking" means a thorough housecleaning, getting rid of all the historical and religious junk so that the unshakable essentials stand clear and uncluttered. Do you see what we've got? An unshakable kingdom! And do you see how thankful we must be? Not only thankful, but brimming with worship, deeply reverent before God. For God is not an indifferent bystander. He's actively cleaning house…"***

God wants His Church, the primary agent of the kingdom, to be unshakable, unassailable, and indivisible. In Matthew 12:25 (KJV), Jesus said, *"Every kingdom divided against itself is brought to desolation; and every city or house divided against itself shall not stand."* We must make sure that we are not promoting *'di-vision'* when it comes to the building of His Church by yielding to our ideas and rejecting His.

When God and man's thinking collide, God's thinking will always override. His thoughts and ways are higher than ours: *"For my thoughts are not your thoughts, neither are your ways my ways, saith the Lord. For as the heaven are higher than the earth, so are my ways higher than your ways, and my thoughts than your thoughts"* (Isa 55:8-9, KJV).

We must align ourselves to His thoughts and His ways so that our path can be blessed. We learn His ways and paths in the house of the Lord: *"Come, let us go up to the mountain of the Lord, to the house of the God of Jacob; and he will teach us of his ways, and we will walk in his paths..."* (Isa 2:3, KJV). Listening and obeying God's thoughts leads us to an understanding of His ways which ultimately helps us get on the right path.

The integrity of what Christ desires to build is important to Him. You will recall that Jesus went into the temple to cleanse it of religious clutter: it had departed from the Father's original intent. His desire was to restore joy in the Father's house and call it back to prayer for all people (Isa 56:7, AMP). That commitment to integrity continues to this day (1 Peter 4:17 – ***"For the time is come that judgment must begin at the house of God: and if it first begins at us, what shall the end be of them that obey not the gospel of God?"*** – KJV).

I find it difficult to believe that God would be so exact in His creation and construction of the universe with its laws, cycles, DNA, design, seeds reproducing after their own kind, stars maintaining clearly defined orbits, etc., and be casual about the construction of His Church.

I find it incredulous that He was so exact in His directions to build an ark, detailed in His instructions to build the tabernacle and temple, and yet, indistinct when it came to building His most precious possession, the Church, leaving us little to no pattern to follow.

Clearly, the people God chooses to use, the message God wants to be proclaimed, the differing circumstances each generation faces, and the methodology God uses to reach nations may change, but it is my conviction that the essential DNA of His House, His Church, does not.

One of the characteristics of divinity is immutability. Man changes, but God does not: He does not have to. I am convinced that there are fundamentals and essentials in everything God builds, and that includes His Church.

Chapter 3
The Until Factor

"In order to realize the worth of the anchor, we need to feel the stress of the storm."
Corrie Ten Boom

"Anything that is unexpected is the X-factor."
Dante Hall

"If you are unable to understand the cause of a problem, it is impossible to solve it."
Naoto Kan, former President of Japan

Jesus taught us that there is a difference between the wise man and the foolish man when it comes to building (Matt 7:24-27). Jesus described two houses that were built: one was built on sand (man's ideas); the other was built on rock (Christ's words). Both the wise man and the foolish man heard the Word of God, but only the wise man heeded and built upon God's wisdom - His promises, precepts, and protocols.

Jesus is speaking to disciples here as the unbeliever would not be cognizant of the Word of God. The wise man and the fool occupy seats in the congregation Sunday morning. Scripture implies that both structures looked good *until* the storm came: the rains fell, the floods rose, and the winds blew (Matt 7:24-29). Only that which was built upon the Rock withstood the storm.

Storms expose any cracks in the foundation, and any church built upon sand – man's ideas, philosophy, culturally shifting fads – will ultimately suffer a complete collapse. We are warned in scripture by Paul that

> ***"we are not carrying on our [spiritual] warfare according to the flesh and using the weapons of man. The weapons of our warfare are not physical [weapons of flesh and blood]. Our weapons are divinely powerful for the destruction of fortresses. We are destroying sophisticated arguments and every exalted and proud thing that sets itself up against the [true] knowledge of God, and we are taking every thought and purpose captive to the obedience of Christ"*** (2 Cor 10:3-5).

This is a significant statement. Our battle is not against **"*flesh and blood*"** but is against theories and ideologies that run contrary to the Word of God. Paul warns us: *"**See to it that no one takes you captive through philosophy and empty deception [pseudo-intellectual babble], according to the tradition [and musings] of mere men, following the elementary principles of this world, rather than following [the truth—the teachings of] Christ**"* (Col 2:8).

Unfortunately, I have watched the Church come and go over fifty years. I have seen success and witnessed monumental failure. Many successes imploded when there was a departure from, or disrespect for the Word of God. How can God back up leaders who disregard or reject building according to His building code? Does God have to? I don't believe so.

Jesus warned His disciples: *"**Not everyone who says to Me, 'Lord, Lord,' will enter the kingdom of heaven, but only he who does the will of My Father who is in heaven**"* (Matt 7:11). The Father's will is found in His Word. Violations of His will – doing our own thing our own way – will ultimately carry with it consequences.

It is the *'until factor'* that concerns me deeply. Men and women give their lives building the Church and advancing the kingdom. Their personal lives may be solidly intact with scriptural principles. However, what is built needs to carry integrity, too, and be aligned to His Word. I have been a minister for close to fifty years now and I have seen good men and women terribly hurt because what has been built – i.e. churches, ministries, missions - could not stand the *'until factors.'*

How does one evaluate the character or integrity of the construction of the Church? If the Church has structurally aligned itself to man-made ideas, how will it stand? If we *'hear His Word'* but *'do not implement His Word,'* or *'replace His Word with our opinions,'* or *'surrender to corporate concepts of best practice according to the world,'* will what has been built sustain spiritual, moral and cultural challenge? We do not want to see the Holy Spirit resisting what we have built and want so desperately to see blessed.

Jesus said He would build His Church, and the gates (strategies, spiritual strongholds, ideologies) of Hell would not be able to overpower or subdue it (Matt 16:18). There are some very clear descriptions as to what comprises the Church He is building.

1. Jesus is the **"Cornerstone of the foundation"** (everything built must be

aligned to Him, for He is the essential part upon which the Church's existence depends): ***"You are fellow citizens with the saints (God's people), and are [members] of God's household, having been built on the foundation of the apostles and prophets, with Christ Jesus Himself as the [chief] Cornerstone…"*** (Eph 2:19-20);

2. the apostles and prophets comprise the ***"foundation"*** built upon solid doctrine and spiritual discernment, understanding that foundations are support structures and largely unseen, using their authority to uphold and strengthen from the bottom up;
3. leaders are referred to as ***"pillars"*** (Gal 2:9);
4. God's people are referred to as ***"living stones"*** (1 Pet 2:5); and
5. the Church together is considered a spiritual building, a holy temple, both a ***"living body"*** and an '***organic organization***,' the ***"habitation – 'the permanent dwelling place' - of the Spirit"*** (Eph 2:20-22).

I personally believe that many of the management concepts and theories on how the Church should be built and governed have been colored by the world's corporate mentality, or the religious world's control mentality. When that occurs, we lose the power of God and His authorization and blessing on what happens within His House (1 Cor 2:2-7, 2 Tim 3:5). The church that man builds upon his own wisdom becomes vulnerable to the *'until factors,'* which all too quickly manifest.

Jesus saw the departure of the Pharisees and Scribes from His Father's intent in His day. He called them out when He cleansed the Temple. In Matthew 23 Jesus delivers the *'eight woes'* to the Judaist system that emerged. At its root, the problem was that man had shifted the Father's intent for His House away from being a **"*house of prayer for all people*"** (Isa 56:7, KJV).

He saw their hypocrisy (Greek hypokritḗs, meaning *'an actor on a stage'*). He observed and stated this: ***"This people honor Me with their lips, but their heart is far away from Me. In vain do they worship Me, for they teach as doctrines the precepts of men"*** (Matt 15:8-9). One of the greatest manifestations of worship is obedience to the known directives of the Lord. When it comes to building His

House, the Church, the *ekklesia*, we must align it to God's precepts, not to man's. I am convinced that only the church built upon obedience to His wisdom and direction will prevail.

My dad always used to say: *"If you are going God's way, He will stop and give you a lift: if you are not, don't expect a lift."* There is a way that seems right to man, but it leads to self-destruction (Matt 7:13). The right way often goes contrary to the crowd – whether that be religious or cultural – but it leads to life.

> ***"Blessed [fortunate, prosperous, and favored by God] is the man who does not walk in the counsel of the wicked [following their advice and example], nor stand in the path of sinners, nor sit [down to rest] in the seat of scoffers (ridiculers). But his delight is in the law of the Lord, and on His law [His precepts and teachings] he [habitually] meditates day and night. He will be like a tree firmly planted [and fed] by streams of water, which yields its fruit in its season; Its leaf does not wither; and in whatever he does, he prospers [and comes to maturity]"*** (Ps 1:1-3).

Chapter 4
The Ekklesia

"But you are a chosen race, a royal priesthood, a holy nation, a people for his own possession, that you may proclaim the excellencies of him who called you out of darkness into his marvelous light. Once you were not a people, but now you are God's people: once you had not received mercy, but now you have received mercy. Beloved, I urge you as sojourners and exiles to abstain from the passions of the flesh, which wage war against your soul"
1 Peter 2:9–11

As we have already learned, the Church's conception and inception is divine. The Church is the result of Christ's architectural design. The Church is empowered by the Holy Spirit and is able to prevail against anything the enemy would throw at it. The Church has counter-measure strategies that will enable it to reach its destiny despite the world system's and hell's efforts to stop its influence. Christ loves the Church and gave His life for the Church, His bride: its very existence, survival and redemptive success is important to Him.

His Church, His Way

When Jesus said *"I will build My Church,"* He used a term familiar to the culture of His day. He was a great Teacher, and He knew how to create a picture of what He was building that would remain in His disciple's minds. The term for Church is the Greek word *ekklesia*. It comes from *ek*, meaning "*out from and to*" and *kaleo*, meaning "*to call*," and has to do with a group of people called out from one place and to another. Much has been said about its application to a 21st Century mindset, both pro and con, but I am convinced this analogy remains applicable to today.

The word *ekklesia* was a political term used around 500 B.C. and coined in the ancient Greek city of Athens, meaning *'an assembly of citizens.'* Regardless of class, citizens of Athens would assemble and declare war, create military strategy, and hold authorities accountable. It was a place where citizens could gather to discuss and influence political decisions. Historically, their meetings moved from once a month to three to four times a month at the time of Christ.

When Alexander the Great rose to power, he established an Empire throughout the Middle East. He did so by establishing hundreds of Greek city states, towns and military centers, and by historian Plutarch's count, many bore his name: e.g. Alexandria/Cairo; Alexandria, Troas, Turkey; Kandahar (Alexandria), Afghanistan; etc. He had

Greek citizens move there to establish the *ekklesia*. Greek government, law, culture, citizenship, even language, dominated where the *ekklesia* was set up.

Jesus said He would build His *ekklesia* and commissioned His disciples to take the Gospel to the nations, set up His Church in every city, and establish the culture, language, laws and customs of the kingdom of God. This word occurs 114 times in the New Testament referring to *"citizens of heaven, an earthly, spiritual government, who are assembled by the Holy Spirit, to meet with Jesus, the Founder and get wisdom for enlarging the influence of the ekklesia in culture."* The Church constituted the parliament of God, and the Word of God was their Magna Carta.

If you look in a modern-day dictionary, church will be described as *"a place of worship, a body of believers worshipping in a particular building"* (dictionary.com). When the world thinks church, they think building, brick, and mortar, but scripture teaches us that God **"dwells not in temples made with hands"** (Acts 17:24,48, Hebrews 9:24, 2 Corinthians 5:1). That is not the Church Jesus conceived. It was much larger in scope and influence. It was far more relational and organic in nature and much more involved, as Christ was, in the transformation of hearts and minds and the reformation of culture.

His Church, His Way

Since the late 19th Century the idea of church as an *ekklesia* has largely been lost and replaced with rescuing people from an evil world and living secluded religious lives with a primary focus on making it to heaven. The Church went from changing the world to adapting to the world, from radical impact to minimal impact, from revolutionary thinking to relevance thinking, and from engaging the world to protecting itself from the world.

We must get back to *ekklesia* thinking and living. The Church has become much more engaged in feeling the pulse of culture and aligning itself with where culture is going. It has become worldly-minded, rather than Word of God-minded. God's Word – His thoughts, ways, and paths – are trans-cultural in nature. The implication of the new creation, where all things become new, forces us to see everything through His lens rather than our own.

The Church must learn to be counter-cultural in nature and invite the world into conformity to God's thoughts and ways, not the other way around (Rom 12:2). Peer pressure needs to be reversed. The Church is supposed to be a manifestation of the kingdom of heaven. Those who come into contact with the *ekklesia* should experience what heaven is going to be like.

The *ekklesia* described by Christ and His

apostles is a very unique expression of kingdom life: the *ekklesia*

- obeys a different King (Jesus, Acts 5:29)
- yields to different laws (the Bible)
- has a different citizenship (Phil 3:20)
- requires active engagement (Heb 10:25)
- speaks a different language (Phil 4:8)
- functions as a covenantal family (1 Cor 11:25)
- acknowledges a different government of leaders in and over their lives (Heb 13:7,17)
- is committed to expanding the influence of Christ globally (Matt 28:18-20) and
- is passionate about being a godly, moral, transformational influence within every sphere of culture (Rom 12:2; Col 2:8).

My friend, Dennis Peacock, in the Statesmen Project training, outlined the qualitative difference between modern church and *ekklesia* thinking:

1. The *ekklesia* challenges the status quo; the church learns to live with status quo
2. The *ekklesia* requires active citizenship, everyone at the gate, everyone making a difference, bringing kingdom life to the community; the church requires Sunday attendance and participation in programs

3. The *ekklesia* trains people for all of life; the church trains people for church life
4. The *ekklesia* thinks transformation of personal life and impact on society; the church often thinks only about their own soul
5. The *ekklesia* thinks disciple building; the church thinks attendance
6. The *ekklesia* thinks bringing heaven to earth; the church thinks getting people to heaven
7. The *ekklesia* thinks the call is to reconcile the world systems to God; the church thinks the call is to personal and individual reconciliation to God alone

The Church, the *ekklesia*, that Jesus said He would build changed and conquered the known world. There is reaction by world authorities in the Book of Acts to the *ekklesia* coming to town through the influence of Paul and Silas: ***"These men who have turned the world upside down have come here too..."*** (17:6). Would to God that every city leader today would have the same response when they see the moral vibrancy and creative relevance of the *ekklesia*.

Paul Maier, in his forward to the book, *How Christianity Changed the World,* by Alvin Schmidt, stated this:

David Kalamen

"With the increasing secularization of society and the current emphasis on multiculturalism — especially in religious matters — the massive impact that Christianity has had on civilization is often overlooked, obscured, or even denied. There is a need to set the record straight…No other religion, philosophy, teaching, nation, movement — whatever — has so changed the world for the better as Christianity has done. Its shortcomings … are far outweighed by its benefits to humanity."

Don Hutchison sent me an article he had just written entitled *Some Trust in Chariots, Status and Celebrity*. What he said was worth noting:

"Christianity was prohibited. But permitted was leaving unwanted infants by the side of the road to die. Particularly unwelcome were girls and babies with visible defects. Christians valued (and value) all life as being created in the image of God (Gen 1:27). Early Christians did not lobby government for change. They set about to rescue as many of the children as they found alive, accepting lifelong responsibility just as they did for brothers and sisters, widows and orphans within the Church. In later centuries the Church established orphanages, adoption agencies, homes for unwed mothers, hospitals, alcohol and addiction recovery homes, schools (from Sunday schools to universities),

inner city missions for those living homeless, halfway houses for men and women released from prison, food banks, and more..."

R. C. Sproul wrote this commentary on our Western culture:

"The church is safe from vicious persecution at the hands of the secularist, as educated people have finished with stake-burning circuses and torture racks. No martyr's blood is shed in the secular west. So long as the church knows her place and remains quietly at peace on her modern reservation. Let the babes pray and sing and read their Bibles, continuing steadfastly in their intellectual retardation. The church's extinction will not come by sword or pillory, but through the quiet death of irrelevance. But let the church step off the reservation, let her penetrate once more the culture of the day and the ... face of secularism will change from a benign smile to a savage snarl."

How is the present, modern-day church doing? The Barna Group, in their online editorial on *Americans Divided on the Importance of Church*, asked,

"What, if anything, helps Americans grow in their faith...people offered a variety of answers—prayer,

family or friends, reading the Bible, having children—but church did not even crack the top 10 list. Although church involvement was once a cornerstone of American life, U.S. adults today are evenly divided on the importance of attending church. While half (49%) say it is "somewhat" or "very" important, the other 51% say it is "not too" or "not at all" important. The divide between the religiously active and those resistant to churchgoing impacts American culture, morality, politics and religion."

God is calling the Church to be the *ekklesia*. G. K. Chesterton said, *"We do not want a church that will move with the world. We want a church that will move the world."* I am not called to go to church, as I am called to be the Church. I am not called to create the church after my own image, but to build the Church according to His image and likeness. It is a *'be'* thing before it is a *'do'* thing. Who we are, representing the Lord Jesus as Christians, re-presencing Him in culture, is the call. What we do flows out of who we are. We are called to be salt and light, to penetrate the corruption and the darkness.

It is clear to me that if we have the ideology of the Church wrong – our ecclesiology – we will attract the world to a man-made concoction of what we believe the Church is supposed to be. It will be powerless and irrelevant. When the Church devolves to the lowest common denominator of modern culture, which is continually refashioning itself based upon feelings, opinion polls and circumstances, it loses its relevance. We experience a *"**form of religion that denies the power of God**"* (2 Tim 3:5, KJV): it literally impedes the manifestation of His glory, His Person, His character, and presence.

The Church that Christ is building is relevant to our present culture only because it supersedes culture with higher thoughts, ways and paths. It draws humanity up to the best expression and representation of God's intention. It is not influenced or controlled by culture, but a primary influencer of culture. The *ekklesia* does not go to the world to define itself through their eyes but goes to the Word to define itself through God's eyes.

It is time that we investigate a new wineskin for the 21st Century church based upon ancient paths. We must unapologetically search out His thoughts, ways and paths. This is the better way, not the easiest way. The Spirit of God is calling the Church back to the Father's original intent. If we get this right, we may see the emergence of a glorious Church, one that our heavenly Father delights in and fills with His presence.

Chapter 5
The Spirit And The Word Speaking Together

"God's word and God's Spirit always agree and are of the same mind. The Spirit of God who gave the Holy Scripture cannot say one thing here and another in your heart. That would be to bear witness against himself. And how can a divided kingdom stand?"
Ralph Venning, from Learning in Christ's School, 1675

"The Spirit and the Word must be combined. If I look to the Spirit alone without the Word, I lay myself open to great delusions also. If the Holy Ghost guides us all, He will do it according to the Scriptures and never contrary to them."
George Muller.

There is a practice that we see repeated in scripture: the Holy Spirit and the Word (Jesus) working in tandem together. For example, in Genesis 1:2 we read **"the Spirit was moving** *upon the face of the waters,"* but it is closely followed by the declaration of the Word of God (*"...and God said"* - vs 3). The Holy Spirit discerned the situation: the Word of God shifted the situation. The creative power of God's Word produced a new system and structure, order out of chaos.

The writer of Hebrews said it this way: *"The Son is the radiance and only expression of the glory of [our awesome] God [reflecting God's Shekinah glory, the Light-being, the brilliant light of the divine], and the exact representation and perfect imprint of His [Father's] essence, holding and maintaining and propelling all things [the entire physical and spiritual universe] by His powerful word [carrying the universe along to its predetermined goal]"* (Heb 1:3). Jesus, the living Word of God, spoke, and creation, structure, and order came into existence.

We see a similar scenario in Ezekiel 37:4. The prophet Ezekiel is carried by the Spirit to discern a situation. What he sees is a valley filled with dry bones. He is told to prophesy to the dry bones, and as He spoke the Word of the Lord, *"there was a noise, and behold a shaking, and the bones came together, bone to his*

bone" (vs 7). What emerged from it was a new entity, a living army, with life and spirit, a new viable structure. The Spirit and Word worked together to bring new life and structure.

In Revelation 3, on three occasions, the phrase is repeated, ***"He who has an ear, let him hear and heed what the Spirit says to the churches"*** (vs 6, 13, 22). Years ago, those listening to what the Spirit was saying to the Church heard messages revealing the identity and ministry of the Godhead. Much more can be flushed out on these movements, but this is the essence of the impact:

- The Jesus Movement revealed Christ as Lord and Saviour and His coming again;
- The Charismatic Movement revealed the personhood of the Holy Spirit; and
- The Apostolic Movement revealed the heart and order that the Father brings.

This last movement brought a revelation of the Father heart of God. It was broadly welcomed and received as we witnessed a culture and generation devolving under the effects of a father deficit. It tied into the last day prophetic declaration of Malachi: ***"He will turn the hearts of the fathers to their children,*** *and the hearts of the children to their fathers [a reconciliation produced by repentance], so that I will not come and strike the land with a curse [of complete destruction]*" (4:6).

The effect of fatherlessness (depicted as a *"curse"* on society) is profound. Statistics fluctuate with time and generations, but these are the most current I found on a basic search on the Internet:

- 63% of youth suicides are from fatherless homes (US Dept. Of Health/Census) – 5 times the average;
- 90% of all homeless and runaway children are from fatherless homes – 32 times the average;
- 85% of all children who show behavior disorders come from fatherless homes – 20 times the average (Center for Disease Control);
- 85% of youths in prison come from fatherless homes;
- 71% of high school dropouts come from fatherless homes, etc.

This message on fathering is very personal to me. My dad's father left him and his mother when he was six months old. His mom, an emigrant from Czechoslovakia, brought up in the Catholic tradition, was born again and filled with the Holy Spirit in the early part of the Pentecostal movement. When she came home, changed by this spiritual encounter, her husband said that she could not love two men. The choice? *'Him'* or *'Jesus.'*

She did her best to convince him that she could love both, and loving Jesus made her more capable of loving him. He rejected that, took them on a holiday to Florida, and on the last day of the holiday he divorced her. My father grew up without a father, as a single child in significant poverty, while his father lived nearby as a very wealthy businessman. What he called *"little mom's"* in the neighbourhood raised him while his mom went to work in New York City for Jewish tailors.

He told the story of his mother encouraging him to go and meet his father at twelve years old. My dad went to the construction site and introduced himself with *"Hi, Pops."* His father turned away from him, saying, *and "Don't you ever call me Pops."* My dad took a piece of wood, created a *'piggy board'* out of it to be used as a bread board. I remember, in his later years, while cleaning out the home in preparation for my mom and dad's transition to new living quarters, seeing this ragged, beaten piece of wood. I was going to throw it out, when Dad stopped me and said, *"It is the only thing my father ever gave me."*

My dad wanted my sister and I to meet his father. One year, while our family was visiting his mom in Perth Amboy, New Jersey, we went to my grandfather's home all dressed up in our Sunday best. When dad knocked on the door and introduced us to my grandfather's common-law wife, she shouted inside and invited him to meet us. I do not have a picture of what he looks like to this day, but I will never forget the sound of his voice when he responded from within: *"Tell them to go away!"*

My father grew up looking for a father. He developed a wonderful relationship to Heavenly Father and became a great man of prayer. However, he always carried what I would call an *'orphan spirit.'* His prayers often bordered on begging God, accompanied by tears, while I approached God as a son with an inheritance mentality. Later, as his life was ending, my dad struggled with very real feelings of rejection and abandonment. I would pray with him and invite the manifestation of the presence of God. The Lord would faithfully presence Himself and peace would come to my dad's soul.

David Kalamen

For years I struggled with our relationship as Monday was pastor's day off and I was in school. Saturday was my day off and Dad was studying for ministry Sunday. My dad was a great visitation pastor, but when I grew up and had a family of my own, he would seldom drop by and visit. I remember struggling with this paradox, asking the Lord what I should do. The Holy Spirit spoke to me clearly: *"You are looking for a father from a man who has never known one. Teach him how to be a father by being a faithful son. Make a draw on his fathering."*

At that stage in life I had become very independent, making all the adult decisions I needed to make for myself and my family. If I lacked wisdom, I sought the advice of my friends who had knowledge I did not. However, from that point on, whether I felt I knew the right decision to make or not, I would call on my dad for wisdom. I spent every Monday faithfully taking him out for breakfast, drawing upon his fathering.

Though I had done everything I felt was possible to bless and honour him – spiritually, morally, educationally – I had never heard him say that he was proud of me. These words children long to hear from their father. The soul often aches for a kind word that recognizes who they are, what they have become, and what they have accomplished. The absence of that affirmation leads children to try and find support from other sources that may or may not be a benefit to their upbringing.

One Sunday, after preaching about true sonship and inviting the *"spirit of sonship"* into our church, there was a revelatory switch in my dad. I had shared that even Christ needed to hear His Father say, **"This is My beloved Son, in whom I am well-pleased"** (Matt 3:17, KJV), even though He had not performed a single miracle up to that point. His value as a Son was not based on works, but on His identity as a Son.

My dad was listening to what the Spirit was saying to the church. Within a few weeks of that message, my dad came up to me and said, *"You are my son in whom I am well-pleased."* He got a revelation of sonship, and never lost it. It was one of the best days of his and my life.

Chapter 6
Reconciling Today's Church To The Ekklesia

"God's Plan: Let's begin, argh, at the beginning."
Iain Gordon, Jesus Plus Nothing, Tauranga, New Zealand

What holds creation together are structures and systems. God governs the universe through laws and He structures their interaction. Since man's fall into sin, humanity has lost its way. Christ was sent to ***"reconcile the world"*** (Greek *kosmos*, the world system and order) to the Father's original intent (2 Cor 5:19) and gave to the Church the message and the ministry of reconciliation to carry on with that eternal purpose.

Scripture affirms that world systems need to be reconciled to the Heavenly Father. We live in an out-of-order environment. The systems and structures have been displaced with other systems and structures affected by broken humanity. We can see that deterioration in the family, in the Church, in the business community, and in the nation. The further we are removed from God's thoughts, ways and paths, the more society devolves into an expression of its worse self (Rom 1). The more godless society becomes, the more systems and structures break down, and the more lawlessness and disorder reigns.

The Church is called to preach repentance, to cause an individual or a generation to turn back to God's original intent, to be reconciled to God personally, and to allow God to restore life, purpose, and structure to their lives. God is not the author of confusion, but of order and peace (1 Cor 14:33, KJV): peace with God, with oneself, and with those around us. It is also a call to yield to new ways of thinking and functioning, new systems and structures, intended to bring healthy outcomes.

If the Church is called to reconcile the world to God's original intent for humanity, to be recreated in God's image, to be transformed through a renewing of the mind, then the Church itself must be willing to be brought back and reconcile itself to God's original intent. Over the centuries, man's thinking has at times displaced God's thinking. Man's thoughts became habit, and habit became tradition, and not all of it has been Biblically based. The Church, its life, order, and structure, needs to be re-aligned and reconciled.

In Matthew 9, Jesus said that new wine must be afforded a new wineskin, or both wine and wineskin will be ruined: *"No one puts a piece of unshrunk (new) cloth on an old garment; for the patch pulls away from the garment, and a worse tear results. Nor is new wine put into old wineskins [that have lost their elasticity]; otherwise, the wineskins burst, and the [fermenting] wine spills and the wineskins are ruined. But new wine is put into fresh wineskins, so both are preserved"* (vs 16-17). The new wine describes what the Spirit is saying, the Word of the Lord, and the new wineskin is the resultant structure that will sustain the integration and application of that Word.

The Holy Spirit has been clear: the world needs to be reconciled to the Heavenly Father. The enemy has attempted to distort and pervert the image of the Father to an entire generation. A return to the heart of the Father is a vital solution to a world facing a father deficit.

The Church received this word and an apostolic movement emerged globally, but on the whole, the local church model of governance did not shift to handle the changes a revelation of apostolic order required. The new wine was poured into old wineskins, and for many, both the new wine was lost, denominational defaults were challenged, and traditional structures were ruined.

Chapter 7
The Apostolic Fathering Movement

"The radical change in the sixteenth century was largely theological. The current reformation is not so much a reformation of faith…but a reformation of practice".
Peter Wagner

That day when my dad shared his heart with me was a defining moment for both of us. In a moment of time, both his father heart and a son's heart were healed. Since that day I dedicated myself to see the *ekklesia*, the Father's House, released in full measure. I committed myself to the apostolic calling, to be a spiritual father to a spiritual family. I knew that it meant saying, *"No!"* to other opportunities to advance up the ecclesiastical ladder of success, from one church to a larger one.

I remain convinced that the *ekklesia* needs to be fathered by spiritual fathers and mothers, the older training the younger, developing spiritual sons and daughters (heirs) who carry the DNA and the hope of an inheritance. That means that the essential makeup of leadership selection and transition needs to be re-evaluated. If a leader wants to be a spiritual father, grow a spiritual family, and pastor a community long-term, something needs to change in the local church paradigm.

Denominational history shows pastoral turnovers at an unprecedented rate. Denominations differ slightly, but the stats are very similar between both the Catholic and Protestant churches. Both pastors and priests move on average every 3.6 years. A quick Google search reveals that in some denominational settings there are one-year appointments (United Methodist Church); in others, pastors can be moved at any time (e.g. Salvation Army).

I bring this up because this attrition rate runs contrary to the intention of the *ekklesia* and the apostolic model. I humbly ask: *"If a family changed mothers and fathers every 3-5 years, would there be generational dysfunction in that nuclear family?"* The Statistics for Canada show that 16.4% of all families are one parent families (1,686,340) - https://www150.statcan.gc.ca/n1/pub/11-627-m/11-627-m2022039-eng.htm). I think that you know the answer.

I am thankful that the leadership and congregation of Kelowna Christian Center opened their heart to the idea of an apostolic leader, a spiritual father, committed to growing old with them. The last forty-two years of my life have been blessed with many spiritual sons and daughters who are passionate about their inheritance.

I ask then, *"If a pastor or spiritual leader is changed every 3-5 years, what kind of dysfunction does that bring to the church?"* There is no perfect church nor are there perfect leaders, just as there are no perfect families or parents. However, imperfection does not imply disqualification. Leaders need help at times; they need healing and restoration, but so too does the church.

The dysfunction in local churches often occurs through the differing mandates and calls resting on numerous, ever-transitioning leaders who are leading the church in different directions. One Board member told me while I was attempting to help them find a new pastor: *"Each pastor has come with a different calling, anointing and vision. We attempted to make each visionary successful, but we just get to see some success and they move on. Now, we say that we are behind them, but way behind them. We have lost the energy."*

Have you ever seen a pastor kept and a church fired? All sin needs to be confronted and addressed, whether in pastors or churches. A pastor can infect a church with compromised leadership, but a church, due to longstanding issues, can be the death knell for every pastor.

Each one's spiritual DNA must be re-aligned to Biblical values which I will expand on later. We need to know what to change, why to change, and what to change to.

God places the solitary in families. That is where we all grow up and mature together. Every mom and dad needs grace to lead a family: every pastor needs grace to lead a church. To those who function in humility, who recognize their need, who see their calling and commit themselves to long-term growth, there is great hope and future.

In this apostolic movement, there was an emphasis on knowing the Father Heart of God. The Holy Spirit was inspiring the Church to experience true fathering so that the Church could be a solution to the world's fatherlessness. An Apostolic movement emerged focusing on the establishment of spiritual fathers in the Church. Organizations like Promise Keepers and numerous apostolic associations were established.

The Spirit moved with revelatory power, the new wine of the Word was released, but in terms of local church structure, a new wineskin substantially remained unformed. As a result, both the new wine (fathering) and the established church structures (governance) have been in jeopardy of failing and breaking. We heard the message of fathering, understood its relevance, taught it and practiced it, but the structure or governance of the Church did not shift or adapt.

It is important that we put *"flesh on bones"* or *"new wine in a new wineskin,"* and bring together *'organic Christianity'* with *'apostolic structure.'* I know that this may be a difficult matter for some of us to process, but I sincerely believe that was the essence of the Spirit's call to the 21st Century *ekklesia*.

Many questions emerge from this potential shift that must be addressed. They are often seen to conflict with each other and are mostly counterproductive. However, I sincerely believe they find their home in an apostolic church model.

- Is our skeletal structure more important than our organic make-up?
- Is superstructure more important than infrastructure?
- Is who we are more important than what we do – being over doing?
- Is relational equity more important than vision casting?
- Is planning and projects more important than people?

From my perspective, with God, it is never an either/or but a both/and issue. All of these questions become mute when we realize that the truth train travels on two tracks and there is perfect balance with who God is and how He functions.

David Kalamen

The Church has struggled for years with what to do with what appears to be contradictory theological positions: e.g. the sovereign will of God and the free will of man; the goodness and the severity of God; the apostolic and the prophetic; etc.

However, truth always constitutes one coin with two distinct sides. Jesus was both 100% Son of God and 100% Son of Man. He was not half and half. He is not 50% wrath and 50% love. The two exist compatibly together, one not affecting the integrity of the other.

From my perspective, my life as a Christian is *'all about Jesus,'* but from God's perspective, it is *'all about me.'* I have learned to live within that paradigm. They are not competing, but completing concepts. Knowing that He views me as *"the apple of His eye"* affects how I view Him.

Regarding the building of the ekklesia, we must see that both the health of organic relationships and the strength of organic structure is of equal importance. That is where my journey took me. It started with asking the Father this question: *"If the Church you build is to be unassailable, and the church must have a wineskin for the new wine, what does this wineskin look like?"* How does the organic message of fathering sync with the way the Church should function and govern?

I sincerely believe that a church is strengthened when they see a spiritual father stand firm against physical, theological and spiritual storms. When they see a willingness of a spiritual father to fight for their inheritance rather than succumb to the pressures to lay down their arms, a church rises. Spiritual fathers see beyond themselves and built for a better future. They realize that the seeds they water today may only bloom long after they are gone.

Chapter 8
The Government Of The Godhead

Government - *"The action or manner of controlling or regulating a nation, organization, or people"* (Oxford Languages Dictionary), *"the act or process of governing"* (Merriam-Webster Dictionary), *"the system used for controlling a country, city, or group of people"* (Cambridge Dictionary)

I began searching the scriptures and was led to study the first government structure in history, the original governance style and substance of the Godhead. I was impressed with how solid the relationship between the Father, Son and Holy Spirit was, and their distinct function. They have eternally worked together as *"us"* (Gen 1:26), and have never had a falling out, an offense, a separation, or failure to achieve.

The Apostle Paul outlined the *'duties of governance'* defined in the Godhead. In 1 Corinthians 12:4-6 (KJV) he says, **"Now there are diversities of gifts, but the same Spirit. And there are differences of administrations, but the same Lord. And**

there are diversities of operations, but it is the same God which works all in all." From what we can assess from these verses:

- The Father is the original cause or the head of operations (Greek *energematon* – activity)
- Christ is the creative power, life giver, and head of administration (Greek *diakonian* – service)
- Holy Spirit is the sustainer and manifesting power of what has been created (Greek *phanerosis* – causing what has been produced to come to the light and shine)

I believe God did leave us a model of apostolic governance, in Himself, and it flows from how the Father, Son and Holy Spirit *'dance together'* (Greek perichoresis – Jn 17:21 – "...***that they all may be one; just as You, Father, are in Me and I in You, that they also may be one in Us, so that the world may believe***..." (KJV). The word perichoresis comes from two Greek words, *peri*, which means *'around,'* and *chorein*, which means *'to give way'* or *'to make room.'* It could be translated *'rotation'* or *'a going around.'* I use the phrase *'dance together.'*

So, what is it like to dance with the Father as Christ and the Holy Spirit do? What holds their relationship together and enables them to continue creating and expanding their influence and governance into an eternal, unshakable, ever-increasing kingdom? I believe that the Godhead invites us to *'dance with them'* – i.e. let them take the lead – and learn what governance looks like from their perspective.

The apostolic model I want to talk about can influence and shape the nuclear family, what the Puritans called *'the little ekklesia,'* fathers and mothers working together with children. It can impact the business and corporate world, where *'employers and employees start functioning as a family'* and work for the good of generations. It can affect the operation and success of cities as *'city fathers work with citizens'* to transform communities. It can work for nations as *'fathers of confederation'* apply the same principles to their oversight of citizens.

I call it an *'apostolic model'* because it was instituted from the Heavenly Father's heart for the Father's House and should function and manifest itself through spiritual fathers and mothers to spiritual heirs, sons and daughters. If pastors, elders, and congregation would function in alignment with the kind of government flowing from the Godhead, the *ekklesia* would be healthy and successful.

The Father is looking for a return on the implementation of His governance style. I know that each region of the world has different secular governmental and denominational requirements for churches and charities. Jesus said in Matthew 22:21, *"...give Caesar what is his, and give God what is His"* (Matt 22:21, Msg).

We have a responsibility to discern the difference, realizing that our accountability is two-fold: to God, first and foremost; and then, to secular Government. KCCS's Organizational chart reflects that, defining both spiritual and governmental priorities, ensuring that operational, educational and administrative roles reflect the appropriate levels of accountability. *"For from Him [all things originate] and through Him [all things live and exist] and to Him are all things [directed]...Amen"* (Rom 11:36).

The government of God is held together through an adherence to *seven essential principles* (not policies). These principles reflect key values which ultimately impact behaviour and success in function. I will not address their co-eternality, co-omnipresence, co-immutability, co-omnipotence, or co-omniscience. These attributes are above us: they make God, God; and they make us, not God.

Suffice it to say this. Paul prayed, *"...that I may know Him [experientially, becoming more thoroughly acquainted with Him, understanding the remarkable wonders of His Person more completely] ...."* (Phil 3:10). We need a growing revelation into who God is. The more we know Him, the more we will grow in our capability to govern as He does. Values like these below will become the norm:

- Unity without uniformity
- Community over individualism
- Authority and submission over independent action
- Relationship empowering function

Values proceed from belief systems. If our belief systems are intrinsically connected to the Word of God and the Godhead's modus operandi, and our worldview is kingdom of God-centered, governance will become organically related to how God does business in and through His Church, the *ekklesia*. Let's take a good look at what these values are and mean to the operation of leadership and governance.

Chapter 9
Seven Essential Values Impacting Governance In The Godhead

"Forasmuch then as we are the offspring of God, we ought not to think that the Godhead is like unto gold, or silver, or stone, graven by art and man's device" (Acts 17:29, KJV)

"For the invisible things of him from the creation of the world are clearly seen, being understood by the things that are made, even his eternal power and Godhead; so that they are without excuse" (Rom 1:20, KJV)

"For in him dwelleth all the fulness of the Godhead bodily" (Col 2:9, KJV)

It is not my purpose to explain the Godhead here as that remains to many a mystery that ultimately will be fully revealed, but scripture is clear: the Father, the Son and the Holy Spirit are all referred to as God.

- The Father is God – ***"For when He received honor and glory from God the Father, such an utterance as this was made to Him by the Majestic Glory, 'This is My beloved Son with whom I am well-pleased'"*** (2 Pet 1:17)
- The Son (Jesus) is God – ***"But of the Son He says, Your throne, O God, is forever and ever, and the righteous scepter is the scepter of His kingdom"*** (Heb 1:8)
- The Holy Spirit is God – ***"But Peter said, 'Ananias, why has Satan filled your heart to lie to the Holy Spirit and to keep back some of the price of land? [...] You have not lied to men, but to God'"*** (Acts 5:3-4)

We read in Genesis 1:1, ***"In the beginning God*** (Hebrew, *Elohim*) ***created the heaven and the earth."*** *"Elohim"* is plural for *"El"*, and many believe it refers to the plurality of the Godhead. Later, in the act of creating humanity, scripture says, ***"And God said, 'let Us make man in Our image, according to Our likeness...'"*** (1:26).

Monotheism (the belief in one deity) was unique to God's people in the Old Testament. Moses said, *"**Hear, O Israel! The Lord is our God, the Lord is one**"* (Deuteronomy 6:4). The Hebrew word for one, *ehad,* speaks of a *'compound unity.'* The Lord said, *"**Remember the former things long past, for I am God, and there is no other; I am God, and there is no one like Me**"* (Isa 46:9). There is nothing we can use to compare to who the Godhead is: there is no one like our God. I do know we can all have a unique and intimate relationship to the Father, to the Son, and to the Holy Spirit.

As I investigated how they dance together, I saw seven shared values that are the root cause of their success. The mystery of the Godhead became practical when it came to understanding relationship and function. I wanted to know if these shared values were transferrable to the function of governance in the 21st Century church.

The Father is the head of operations. These values were set as the operational priority between them. Both the Lord Jesus and the Spirit yielded to these seven values. If they did, I can, and will. If they were successful in guiding them governmentally and operationally, I believe they will be for me. This is how God does business with Himself. These values are the guardrails He uses to get the work done. They are the divine plumb line that govern all activity.

If we are going to dance together with God, then we must concentrate on making what is important to the Godhead important to us. Just as natural sons and daughters mimic and express the values of parents, spiritual sons and daughters must learn from our Heavenly Father, our elder brother, Jesus, and the Person of the Holy Spirit.

Let's look at these governing values that I am referring to as critical pieces of apostolic government.

First: The Value Of Authority

There has to be a Head and the Father has been defined and described as such in the Godhead. The three Persons of the Godhead are co-equal: submission to authority does not imply inequality or inequity. Both the Son and the Spirit submit to the Father's authority (Jn 14:28 – ***"My Father is greater than I"***).

The government of God starts with a recognition of Who is in authority. This authorization flows from ***"His throne"*** (Rev 22:1). There is clearly submission to the will of the Father in Christ (Jn 5:30 – ***"I can do nothing on my own initiative or authority"***), and to the will of Christ by the Spirit (Jn 14:26 –

"He will teach you all things and help you remember everything that I have told you"). This submission to authority does not mean inequality, but it expresses *'uniqueness in functionality.'*

Apostolic government rises and falls on whether there is authority, and who is recognized as such. Authority in the *ekklesia* must truly and authentically reflect the authority of the Person of the Father. Christ's ministry was all about revealing and introducing a true reflection of the Father to humanity: He was sent by the Father to reveal the Father in human form, to fulfill the will of His Father, and to teach humanity how to have a relationship with the Father like He had.

Jesus received power and authority to function from His Father (Rev 2:27). When Christ's work was done, He asked the Father and the Father authorized that the Holy Spirit be sent to complete and bring to fruition what Jesus started (Jn 14:16).

The Apostles were appointed to take a revelation of the Father, not just the Gospel, to the nations. The early Church Fathers were responsible to *'represent'* (re-presence) the Father, just as Christ did, answering Thomas when he asked to see the Father: **"Anyone who has seen Me has seen the Father"** (Jn 14:9). No governance in the *ekklesia* can survive without a recognition of God-appointed and anointed authority.

There is no recorded rebellion within the Godhead towards the Heavenly Father's authority in scripture. It was a holy authority, and worthy of submission. All throughout scripture the chorus of praise goes up to the Father honouring His goodness in the exercise of His authority: *"Worthy are You, our Lord and God, to receive the glory and the honor and the power; for You created all things, and because of Your will they exist, and were created and brought into being"* (Rev 4:11).

Second: The Value Of Covenant

Covenant is a Biblical term. It far exceeds the idea of a contract. It is a mutually binding, all-embracing commitment, a coming together for a common purpose between two or more parties. In Hebrews 6:13 the writer states that *"when God made the promise to Abraham, He swore [an oath] by Himself, since He had no one greater by whom to swear."*

God is a covenant making and keeping God. It is seen in one of the first acts of creation: Jeremiah spoke of the covenant of the day and the night that no one can alter (33:19-20). Who was God covenanting to if humanity had not even been created yet? He was covenanting to Himself, and because there was no one else to swear to, He swore an oath to Himself.

The Old Testament is filled with illustrations of God's covenantal nature. Man can break covenant with God and each other, but God's covenant is established in the heavens. Even when man sinned, God did not go back on His covenant to create a solution. *"He has remembered his covenant for ever, the word which He commanded to a thousand generations"* (Ps 105:8). The strength of the government of the Godhead is their commitment to each other, to their nature, their value system and their word.

The Father, Son and Holy Spirit are in covenant with each other and will not sully their character by going back on a covenantal promise. *"If we are faithless, He remains faithful [true to His word and His righteous character], for He cannot deny Himself"* (2 Tim 2:13).

God is all-knowing, so nothing that He has promised conflicts with what He already knows. He is all-powerful, so nothing He has purposed is unable to be performed. He is immutable and does not have to change His promise to Himself or humanity. He is a covenant-making and covenant-keeping God.

I believe that this is what attracted the Heavenly Father's heart with King David. David loved to praise and create songs about God and life, but he also carried some significant moral defects. We know that when he sinned, and was found out, he was humble and contrite. So, when God found a man after his own heart, what was the attraction? I believe it was David's covenantal nature, shown towards King Saul, Jonathan, Mephibosheth, and others.

Three: The Value Of Unity

Though the Godhead remains *"diverse in function and gifting,"* they remain *"one in purpose"* (their diversity is a strength). They are three in one, inseparably united. Nothing proceeds from independent motivation: there are no hidden or private agendas. Each are submitted to the whole intent and plan agreed upon.

This unity was spoken of by Christ in John 17, what I have referred to as the *"perichoresis of God"* (the dance). **"I do not pray for these alone [it is not for their sake only that I make this request], but also for [all] those who [will ever] believe and trust in Me through their message, that they all may be one; just as You, Father, are in Me and I in You, that they also may be one in Us, so that the world may believe [without any doubt] that You sent Me"** (vs 20-21).

There is great power in unity. When God saw what was happening to men's hearts after the Fall, He intervened: *"Behold, they are one [unified] people, and they all have the same language. This is only the beginning of what they will do [in rebellion against Me], and now no evil thing they imagine they can do will be impossible for them. Come, let Us (Father, Son, Holy Spirit) go down and there confuse and mix up their language, so that they will not understand one another's speech"* (Gen 11:6-7). The Godhead is aware of the possibility and capability of unified effort, for both good for evil.

There is no *'di-vision'* in the Godhead (two visions) or independent agenda. They are committed to each other, to the Father's eternal purpose, to their internal value system, and to the outworking of the plan *"when [in God's plan] the proper time had fully come, God sent His Son…"* (Gal 4:4).

Four: The Value Of Honour

The Godhead is the original example of what it means to honour. The Hebrew connotation for honour is regarding someone as being weighty, or as amounting to something. The Greek connotation refers to attributing value and esteem to someone. That sounds great, but it misses the mark regarding the operation of the Godhead.

Within the Godhead, each are honoured because of their intrinsic value. It is not based on subjectivity or opinion. Honour flows from an understanding of their innate worth. Because of their shared attributes and character, to dishonour one would be to dishonour all.

Honour is not attributed because of some achievement or because of what they have done. It hangs on their commitment to be integrous, authentic, and faithful to who they are. They are honourable, and so, they are worthy of honour.

Honour is not self-designated or determined: Jesus said in John 5:23; 8:54: ***"If I glorify Myself, My glory is [worth] nothing. It is My Father who glorifies Me."*** Christ honored His Father, His authority, and exemplified that honor to us, learning obedience through the things He suffered as a son. The Spirit honours what the Son has died to create and administrates that mutual legacy. They honour one another, and so, reap it towards themselves.

This is a huge part of the dance within the Godhead. Their relationship to each other created a culture or atmosphere of honour. No wonder heaven will be a reflection of that when we join the angels, who have seen this constant expression, and sing together: *"**Worthy are You, our Lord and God, to receive the glory and the honor and the power; for You created all things, and because of Your will they exist, and were created and brought into being**"* (Rev 4:11).

Five: The Value Of Love For One Another

There is no question: the Father, Son and Spirit love each other. *"**The one who does not love has not become acquainted with God [does not and never did know Him], for God is love. [He is the originator of love, and it is an enduring attribute of His nature]**"* (1 Jn 4:8). God's love, mercy and grace resonates all through scripture. Nothing makes sense unless the *'love of God'* rules and reigns in life. God, who is the embodiment of love itself, demonstrates that within the Godhead.

John, the disciple whom he said Jesus loved (Jn 13:23), wrote in his gospel the most about love. *"**For the Father dearly loves the Son and shows Him everything that He Himself is doing; and the Father will show Him greater works than these, so that you** *will be filled with wonder"* (Jn 5:20).

In John 14:30-31, Jesus said, *"...the ruler of the world (Satan) is coming. And he has no claim on Me [no power over Me nor anything that he can use against Me]; but so that the world may know [without any doubt] that I love the Father, I do exactly as the Father has commanded Me [and act in full agreement with Him]."*

One may ask about the expression of love in the Person of the Holy Spirit. I am glad that you asked. According to Galatians 5:22, *"The fruit of the Holy Spirit is love."* In other words, the Holy Spirit, who is God, is love itself, and can give away what He is. When you come into a relationship to the Holy Spirit, you encounter the very manifestation of the love of God. Just as Christ gave us insight into the will and intentions of the Father, the Holy Spirit gives us insight into the heart motivation and emotions of the Father.

Love existed between them all *"before the foundation of the world"* (Jn 17:24). This is not an emotional or flippant expression dependant upon moods and circumstances. This is the pro-active decision of the Godhead towards each other. The agape love is unmotivated by the value or worth of the object of love. Its function adds worth to the object of His affection.

His Church, His Way

There is a wonderful portion of scripture in Ephesians 3:16-19. Paul meant it as a prayer, and I pass it on:

"May He grant you out of the riches of His glory, to be strengthened and spiritually energized with power through His Spirit in your inner self, [indwelling your innermost being and personality], so that Christ may dwell in your hearts through your faith. And may you, having been [deeply] rooted and [securely] grounded in love, be fully capable of comprehending with all the saints (God's people) the width and length and height and depth of His love [fully experiencing that amazing, endless love]; and [that you may come] to know [practically, through personal experience] the love of Christ which far surpasses [mere] knowledge [without experience], that you may be filled up [throughout your being] to all the fullness of God [so that you may have the richest experience of God's presence in your lives, completely filled and flooded with God Himself]."

The Godhead has practiced loving each other in such a real way that *'dancing with them'* will draw us into a similar experience with how wide, long, high, or deep His love truly is. God is love. God doesn't just have an emotion called love. He is the very essence of love. If you want to know true love, you will have to get to know God. Only then will you have the capacity to pass it on.

Six: The Value Of Integrity

The dictionary from *Oxford Languages* describes integrity as:

- the quality of being honest and having strong moral principles;
- the state of being whole and undivided;
- the condition of being unified, unimpaired, or sound in construction; and
- having internal consistency or lack of corruption.

The Godhead is the essence of integrity: morally righteous, holy, unified, and consistent. What one member of the Godhead does reflects the character of all three of them. The Godhead has gone to great lengths to be an exact expression of who God is. We read of Christ as being **"the** *exact representation and perfect imprint of His [Father's] essence"* (Heb 1:3).

Jesus said to the Pharisees who asked, *"**Where is this Father of Yours?**" Jesus answered, "**You know neither Me nor My Father; if you knew Me, you would know My Father also**"* (Jn 8:19). How blessed the *ekklesia* is to know that the Church's primary authority is unblemished with compromise, uncorrupted by a sinful nature, or unbroken by a life of lies and pretensions.

God is Holy: He is whole, and He calls us to Himself so that we too can come to wholeness by becoming holy. God is righteous: He is morally clean and calls us to Himself to walk righteously. God is consistent: He is faithful to Who He is and He will not deny His own character. This kind of integrity rules the Godhead in their interaction with each other and humanity.

Integrity – i.e. living according to strict moral and ethical principles, functioning with soundness of moral character, free from corrupting influence or motive, honest in nature, whole, incapable of being diminished, sound, unimpaired, incorruptible, and totally uncompromised – marks who God is and should be the mark of who His family is.

David Kalamen

Seven: The Value Of Adherence To His Own Word

We say things that we should not say. We promise things that we cannot fulfill. We make statements that we cannot back up. We state as fact things that are false conclusions. We tell others to function in a certain way, but we go our own way. This is evidence of broken humanity and why we need a relationship to God, along with a new nature, mind and heart.

The Godhead has a high degree of confidence in the declaration of their word. They have pre-thought their statements, can back up what they say, and honour what they communicate. *"The words and promises of the Lord are pure words, like silver refined in an earthen furnace, purified seven times"* (Ps 12:6). *"The word of the Lord is tested [it is perfect, it is faultless] ..."* (Ps 18:30).

A person's word is only as good as their character. We have already spoken of the Godhead's integrity. It applies to the spoken word. God stands behind His word as strongly as when He spoke and said, *"Let there be light, and there was light"* (Gen 1:3). The Psalmist wrote: *"Forever, O Lord, Your word is settled in heaven [standing firm and unchangeable]"* (119:89).

The testimony of prophecy in the Old Testament confirms to us God's commitment to bring His Word to fulfillment: *"**He has remembered His covenant forever, the word which He commanded and established to a thousand generations**"* (Ps 105:8). God remembered His promises to Israel and sent a deliverer. The numerous prophecies regarding Christ's coming were all fulfilled in the life of Christ, who yielded to the timing of the Father, both in His birth and in His death.

I find it interesting that what the Father said in the Old Testament, Jesus reiterated in the New Testament. What Jesus said in the New Testament, the disciples reiterated in the Book of Acts. What the apostles spoke in the Book of Acts, the Holy Spirit faithfully reiterates today. The Godhead honours the word spoken.

It is so important that Christ is described as the very expression of the word of God: *"**In the beginning [before all time] was the Word (Christ), and the Word was with God, and the Word was God Himself. He was [continually existing] in the beginning [co-eternally] with God**"* (Jn 1:1-2).

God cannot be separated from His Word. His integrity is intertwined with His promises, and they are *'Yes and Amen'* to those who will believe: *"**For as many as are the promises of God, in Christ they are [all answered] 'Yes.' So,**"*

through Him we say our 'Amen' to the glory of God'" (2 Cor 1:20).

Knowing God is one thing; knowing what He has said is another. Faith is simply knowing God well enough that we have confidence that He will back up His word with signs following – a manifestation of the power of His promise.

My Conviction Of Faith

The values I have described above holds the Godhead together, making them integral, functional and impactful:

1. recognition of authority
2. commitment to covenant
3. unity in diversity
4. honour for one another
5. love for one another
6. integrity; and
7. adherence to the Word

I am convinced that these values are critical to the success of the government of God. They are the organic pieces that make up the living structure for how God gets things done. They are the significant keys on the chain that release the kingdom of God. They are vital parts to whether leadership in an organization will fulfill God's intent and purpose.

When these seven values are committed to as a matter of principle, not just policy, by the *ekklesia*, or extensions of His Church, there is a possibility of success and significance. When these values are integrated into family life, the home will flourish. When they are integrated into corporate operations, God's Hand of blessing comes upon a business. When city fathers capture the essence of these values, a city can be saved.

When these values are esteemed as a divine plumb line for vision casting, decision making, and operations, the *ekklesia* will thrive, not just survive. Rebellion, breaking covenant, division, dishonour, offence, compromise, and dissing the word of God are all catalysts for the loss of the anointing and blessing of the Lord.

You can see much of this alluded to in Paul's description of the "perilous times" of the last days:

"....in the last days, dangerous times [of great stress and trouble] will come [difficult days that will be hard to bear]. For people will be lovers of self [narcissistic, self-focused], lovers of money [impelled by greed], boastful, arrogant, revilers, disobedient to parents, ungrateful, unholy and profane, [and they will be] unloving [devoid of natural human

affection, calloused and inhumane], irreconcilable, malicious gossips, devoid of self-control [intemperate, immoral], brutal, haters of good, traitors, reckless, conceited, lovers of [sensual] pleasure rather than lovers of God, holding to a form of [outward] godliness (religion), although they have denied its power [for their conduct nullifies their claim of faith]" (2 Tim 3:1-5)

The power is not in the information presented: it is in the application. Practically, this information must become a revelation of the heart, a conviction and not just a convenience. That revelation must affect us individually first and our lives experience a transformation, taking us on a different spiritual trajectory. Personal transformation will always lead to reformation, where beliefs, systems and structures are changed within organizations and culture.

Chapter 10
Placing Ourselves In Remembrance

"He created the church to meet your five deepest needs: a purpose to live for, people to live with, principles to live by, a profession to live out, and power to live on. There is no other place on earth where you can find all five of these benefits in one place."
Rick Warren

"We need to stop giving people excuses not to believe in God. You've probably heard the expression 'I believe in God, just not organized religion'. I don't think people would say that if the church truly lived like we are called to live."
Francis Chan

What does the local church governance look like when these principles are applied? It should result in a God-ordained shift in spiritual and leadership culture. The way we do business should change from religious practice to righteous practice. A lot has to do with a shift of *'ideology'* and *'philosophy,'* anything at odds with obedience to the truth.

"For the weapons of our warfare are not carnal, but mighty through God to the pulling down of strong holds; casting down imaginations, and every high thing that exalts itself against the knowledge of God, and bringing into captivity every thought to the obedience of Christ..." (2 Cor 10:4-5)

Here are a few thoughts on the practical functionality of these values that govern the Godhead. Each one could be significantly enlarged upon and provide invaluable insight into the way leaders organically are chosen, relate and make visionary decisions. I will outline them as statements of belief.

The Ekklesia Is His House, Not Our house

The Old Testament refers to the building of the Father's House. The key characteristics, found in Isaiah 56:7, were prayer and joy: *"All these I will bring to My holy mountain and make them joyful in My house of prayer...for My house will be called a house of prayer for all the peoples."* One of the first insights into Christ's journey was His visit to the Temple. His reasoning resonates with me as key to our own sense of purpose: *"**Did you not see and know that it is necessary [as a duty] for Me to be in My Father's house and [occupied] about My Father's business?**"* (Lu 2:49).

If one reads Exodus 26 they will see God establishing the outer design for what the Tabernacle looked like. It was *'His House,'* where *'His presence'* would reside. It was where the people could find Him. Everything He designed had a specific function and purpose, and what was built was key to the kind of spiritual meaning Israel was meant to experience.

The Father would draw people to His House. The building of the Tabernacle was a progressive and revelatory step. It would emerge at a higher revelation of God's purpose with David who placed the tent with the ark of His presence on Mount Zion, allowing full access to His presence. It was this act that the Father affirmed as His fullest intent when He promised to *"**raise up and restore the fallen tabernacle of David**"* (Amos 9:11).

A respect for a physical house would be replaced with a desire and opportunity for access to His presence, the greater good. Today we have unusual access: *"**For where two or three are gathered in My name [meeting together** *as My followers], I am there among them"* (Matt 18:20). The spiritual house has replaced the physical house.

When we gather, we comprise both individually and corporately, His House: *"Do you not know and understand that you [the church] are the temple of God, and that the Spirit of God dwells [permanently] in you [collectively and individually]"* (1 Cor 3:16)?

That is why communion is of such importance. It is God's way of keeping His House clean by keeping the hearts of His people clean. It is the Lord's supper, not ours: it is His broken body and shed blood, not ours (1 Cor 11:20). Unworthy participation in this, refusing to acknowledge the Body of Christ, His Church, opens the door to discipline and judgement.

Communion with Christ and each other creates true fellowship and the emergence of a spiritual community. The Father's word rules in His House and at His table. He sits as the Head of His family. We would do well to remember that. Many times, my prayer before the Board or Apostolic team, was preceded by welcoming the Head of the Church to the Chair of the Board. We are to do *'His business, His way.'*

His House Requires The Emergence Of Spiritual Fathers

It is vital that the ekklesia see the emergence of spiritual fathers who carry the apostolic calling and are dedicated to representing (or, re-presencing) the mind and heart or Person of the Father. One might say that Jesus never carried that title of Father with His disciples: teacher, rabbi, yes. However, Christ had two purposes in His coming: to introduce and reconcile the world to their Heavenly Father; and to represent His Father's will and person perfectly.

Jesus told His disciples: *"Have I been with you for so long a time, and you do not know Me yet, Philip, nor recognize clearly who I am? Anyone who has seen Me has seen the Father. How can you say, 'Show us the Father?'"* (Jn 14:9). Jesus, as Head of the *ekklesia*, was giving them an example of how the Father wants things done in His House. The writer of Hebrews (1:3) says:

"The Son is the radiance and only expression of the glory of [our awesome] God [reflecting God's Shekinah glory, the Light-being, the brilliant light of the divine], and the

exact representation and perfect imprint of His [Father's] essence, and upholding and maintaining and propelling all things [the entire physical and spiritual universe] by His powerful word [carrying the universe along to its predetermined goal]."

Paul, the author of the greatest part of the New Testament, was the best illustration of this calling. His apostolic calling was constantly challenged. You hear the pain in his heart in 2 Corinthians 10:12-14:

"We do not have the audacity to put ourselves in the same class or compare ourselves with some who [supply testimonials to] commend themselves. When they measure themselves by themselves and compare themselves with themselves, they lack wisdom and behave like fools.
We, on the other hand, will not boast beyond our proper limit, but [will keep] within the limits of our commission (territory, authority) which God has granted to us as a measure, which reaches and includes even you. We are not overstepping the limits of our province, as if we

did not [legitimately] reach to you, for we were the [very] first to come even as far as you with the good news of Christ."

Paul affirms to Timothy, his spiritual son, his commitment to apostolic function and behaviour towards the *ekklesia* in Thessalonica:

"Even though we had some standing as Christ's apostles, we never threw our weight around or tried to come across as important, with you or anyone else. We weren't standoffish with you. We took you just as you were. We were never patronizing, never condescending, but we cared for you the way a mother cares for her children.... with each of you we were like a father with his child, holding your hand, whispering encouragement, showing you step-by-step how to live well before God" (1 Thess 2:6-7.11, Msg)

He wrote particularly to the Corinthian church, a Christian community conflicted with many moral compromises, speaking to their heart as a spiritual father, exhorting them to listen. He said, *"For even if you were to have ten thousand teachers [to guide you] in Christ, yet you would not have many fathers [who led you to Christ and assumed responsibility for you], for I became your father in Christ Jesus through the good news [of salvation]"* (1 Cor 4:15-16).

No one is born again of the will of man. No one can declare themselves someone's spiritual father. One *'becomes'* a father in Christ through the Gospel. It is the **"*Spirit and the Bride*"** who say, **"*Come*"** (Rev 22:17, Amp). Both the Spirit and the Bride, the *ekklesia*, and those who preach the Word of God have a role in the salvation of the lost. Sons and daughters emerge from the spiritual bond produced through the relationship created by the Word of God.

The question of spiritual fathering is a critical one. This is not a plea to go back to a Catholic form of priesthood, or to form a Protestant fatherhood. It is a plea to rise to another level of spiritual expectation where spiritual leaders begin to think of fathering the *ekklesia* through long term commitment and growing old with a spiritual family.

The Role Of The Apostolic And Fatherly Function Is To Build A Spiritual Family

Spiritual fathers and mothers are called to reproduce spiritual sons and daughters (*"a godly offspring"* - Mal 2:15) who become fathers and mothers themselves. Their role is to generate an inheritance mentality and establish a multi-generational influence.

There are many terms being used in this generation and culture to describe various influencers: life coaches, mentors, disciplers, influencers, etc. None of this compares with the calling to father or mother the *ekklesia*. You can do all of that without relationship, without geographical proximity, but not spiritual fathering.

Much can be said about the differences, far more than this playbook permits. However, if I was to distinguish between these methodologies, I would say this as simply as I can:

- *Disciplers* focus on information, formation of character and accountability
- *Mentors* focus on practical training, example and gifting
- *Fathers* focus on relational equity, calling, life purpose and destiny

My sole objective as an apostolic father is not just to *"**make disciples**"* (Matt 28:19), but to raise and release sons and daughters who are disciplined believers and capable of multi-generational influence. 2 Timothy 2:2 states *"**The things [the doctrine, the precepts, the admonitions, the sum of my ministry] which you have heard me teach in the presence of many witnesses, entrust [as a treasure] to reliable and faithful men who will also be capable and qualified to teach others.**"*

The entire question of whether spiritual leaders will accept the call to fathering is a large one. This is not a title that one seeks, but a life and lifestyle one seeks to live. However, it could be equally asked whether there is a desire within the modern church for parishioners, congregants, or members to move into sonship.

We know that the *"**Spirit of sonship**"* is active in the *ekklesia* to elevate our relationship to God from converts to sons (Rom 8:15), but does that Spirit of sonship continue to build the desire for sonship to an earthly spiritual father? All I know is that the move from being an orphan and a slave to a son is a spiritual journey worth the taking.

The Apostle Paul testified to the rarity of finding a spiritual son when he wrote Timothy these words: *"**I hope in the Lord Jesus to send Timothy to you soon, so that**"*

I may also be encouraged by learning news about you. For I have no one else [like him who is] so kindred a spirit who will be genuinely concerned for your [spiritual] welfare. For the others [who deserted me after my arrest] all seek [to advance] their own interests, not those of Jesus Christ. But you know of Timothy's tested worth and his proven character, that he has served with me to advance the gospel like a son serving with his father..." (Phil 2:19-22).

I am convinced that it is sons that come into the inheritance. The Church must move from seeing themselves as servants, to seeing themselves as sons who serve. *Two scriptural illustrations* come to mind:

- Elijah's transition of anointing and destiny to Elisha (2 Ki 2). Elijah's time of departure was close. He took Elisha to three places – Bethel, Jericho, and the Jordan. Each time he asked Elisha to remain. Each time there were sons of the prophets watching the process. The implication was they were in schools of the prophets. There were many *students*, but there was only one *son*. The students were willing to watch from afar, but the son remained close. When Elijah was taken Elisha cried out, "**My father,** *my father"* (vs 12). A son received the mantle, the prophetic inheritance, and a destiny that was supercharged with miracles.

- Christ's transition into ministry and His inheritance spoken of in Psalm 2:8: *"Ask of Me, and I will assuredly give [You] the nations as Your inheritance."* For thirty years Christ's ministry was serving His earthly family. Then there was a step of obedience into baptism by John (Matt 3:17). *"This is My beloved Son, in whom I am well-pleased and delighted."* That declaration of sonship opened the door to great challenges in the wilderness. Satan poses three temptations strategically, often beginning with the preface: *"If you are the Son of God"* (Matt 4:3, 6). Jesus passed the test of sonship, yielding to His Father, and went into the synagogue and read aloud from Isaiah 61. He was able to access His inheritance and began His ministry.

God wants more than disciples: He wants sons and daughters. God wants more than servants and students: He wants sons and daughters. Sons and daughters carry an inheritance mentality. They are heirs of God, joint heirs with Christ. They see the *ekklesia* differently. They see destiny there.

His Church, His Way

You may ask: *"How many sons and daughters can a spiritual father be relationally connected to?"* We know that there are limitations within a nuclear family. Jesus had twelve disciples, three of which were close to Him (Peter, James, and John), but the closest was John. They went everywhere with Him. They knew Him, heard His words, learned from His example, and saw His works.

The purpose of every natural father is not to raise dependants, but sons and daughters who can raise sons and daughters. There are many sons and daughters in my life that have transitioned to fathers and mothers themselves. There are those who are sons and daughters through the gospel, and there are sons and daughters who make a draw on my fathering. I leave that to the Lord.

It is not about a title. I have no one who calls me *"Father Dave."* I have a number who I have become their spiritual father through the gospel. I have some who refer to me as their spiritual father or *"Papa Dave."* I have many who draw upon my fathering. What I do know is that as I have natural children in my heart in prayer, so God places spiritual sons and daughters in my heart in prayer. What I do know is that when true sons and daughters ask for counsel or draw upon my fathering, an inheritance is poured out of blessing, wisdom, healing, prophetic understanding, and destiny.

Chapter 11
A Church Model Built Upon The Values Of The Godhead

"Our value is the sum of our values"
Joe Batten

Building the local ekklesia based upon the values of the Godhead works. What makes the Godhead functional and successful makes the *ekklesia* functional and successful. God never requires His leaders to do what He is not doing. As Jesus was committed to doing what He saw the Father doing, so must the *ekklesia*. (Jn 5:19 - ***"I assure you and most solemnly say to you, the Son can do nothing of Himself [of His own accord], unless it is something He sees the Father doing; for whatever things the Father does, the Son [in His turn] also does in the same way")***.

The seven essential elements of the Godhead's governmental DNA must be *'taught and caught'* within the ekklesia. They become a moral compass for all action and function. As these values defined God to Himself, they define us to ourselves.

Authority Needs To Be Clearly Defined

Authority represents the Father in His House. There will be an accounting by leaders to the Father for how they handle and exercise that authority and take care of His House: Peter charges leaders to *"exercise oversight not under compulsion, but voluntarily, according to the will of God; and not [motivated] for shameful gain, but with wholehearted enthusiasm; not lording it over those assigned to your care [do not be arrogant or overbearing], but be examples [of Christian living] to the flock [set a pattern of integrity for your congregation]"* (1 Pet 5:2-3).

As Christ was authorized to lead the apostles in the early Church, so leaders need to be authorized by the Father to lead the 21st Century Church. Ordination to leadership comes by the Hand of the Lord: *"Promotion comes neither from the east, nor from the west, nor from the south. God is the judge: He puts down one and sets up another"* (Ps 75:6-7, KJV). No group of people can ordain anyone: they can only recognize those whom the Lord has ordained to lead.

Every *ekklesia* must have a clear perspective on who is in authority under the Lord. God doesn't call committees or Boards: He calls individuals, men and women, then surrounds them as He did Saul with *"**brave men** (and women) **whose hearts He touched**"* (1 Sam 10:26).

In the wilderness David was surrounded by those who were in debt, discouraged and discontent, but they had one thing in common: they recognized that David had been anointed to be the next king of Israel by Samuel. The Bible says that *"**they became mighty men**, **and scripture says that** "**now these are the chiefs of David's mighty men, who strongly supported him in his kingdom, together with all Israel, to make him king, in accordance with the word of the Lord concerning Israel**"* (1 Ch 11:10).

Even Jesus had a team, albeit somewhat dysfunctional, but they had one thing in common: they recognized Christ's authority to lead. By serving the Lord, listening to His counsel and wisdom, watching His ways, they became leaders who were willing to give their lives for who they believed in and what He stood for. The nations were impacted by their obedience.

I saw that occur within Kelowna Christian Center's leadership and their commitment to my authority. As the Lord opened doors of utterance to me apostolically among the nations, God increased their own measure of anointing and authority, giving them significant national and global spheres of influence.

A Commitment To Unity Must Be Seen On All Levels

The principle of unity is well-ingrained within the early Church: a cursory reading of the Book of Acts sees repeated use of the phrases one mind, one heart, one Father, one Spirit, one Lord, and one accord (Acts 5:12, 8:6). The Church was strongest and most effective when it was unified. John Hagee said: *"A church can be unified in one of two ways. You can freeze together, as the church of The Frozen Chosen; or you can melt together with the fire of The Holy Spirit."*

The blessing of unity in leadership is espoused in Psalm 133: unity releases the anointing from the head (leadership) down, opens heaven and releases the commanded blessing of the Lord. When leaders in the Church function like the Godhead functions, there is blessing. Praying until we are in agreement is the hard route to go (**"it seems good to us and the Holy Spirit"** – Acts 15:28), but majority votes often lead to a *'di-vision'* in leadership that create a split.

When Mom and Dad are in unity, the children cannot manipulate and peace comes to the family. When spiritual leadership strive for unity as the scripture exhorts, there is unity in the *ekklesia*: **"Make every effort to keep the oneness of the Spirit in the bond of peace [each individual working together to make the whole successful]"** (Eph 4:3).

In numerous congregational or membership meetings, when vision was proposed and decisions had to be reached by the whole, the question was asked: *"Is leadership in agreement?"* That was the defining question. I can honestly say that agreement released peace. I will say more about that later.

A Culture Of Honour Must Be Cultivated

Honor must be directed *upward* towards God and outward, to His House, the *ekklesia*. There is an interesting verse in Malachi 1:6 where God questions Israel about the honour due Him: **"Isn't it true that a son honors [at least he is supposed to do so] his father and a worker his master? So, if I'm your Father, where's My honor?"** As Jesus honored the Father and the Holy Spirit honored the Son, God is watching whether the culture of the Godhead is reflected in His people's honor.

Honor must be directed *inwardly* as we are incapable of honor towards the Lord or others *outwardly* if we are not honorable towards ourselves. 1 Corinthians 12:29 cautions us to honor every member of the Body of Christ: *"I want you to think about how this keeps your significance from getting blown up into self-importance. For no matter how significant you are, it is only because of what you are a part of"* (Msg).

Paul exhorted the Roman church to *"be devoted to one another in brotherly love. Honour one another above yourselves. Never be lacking in zeal, but keep your spiritual fervour, serving the Lord"* (Rom 12:10-11, NIV). Our personal value is lodged in Christ and in our relationship to His family, the Body of Christ. It is seen in how we treat the least amongst us and the most vulnerable.

The devolution of society is described in Romans 1. The precedent for its demise, deterioration and self-destruction, is seen in verse 21: *"they knew God but did not honor Him as God or give Him thanks."*

God promised great blessing to Eli in 1 Samuel 2, stating that *"his house would go in and out before Him forever"* (vs 30), but because he *"honored his sons above the Lord,"* allowing them to do whatever they wanted in His House, God said, *"be it far from Me"* (vs 30b). He concluded: *"Those who honor Me I will honor, and those who despise Me shall be lightly esteemed"* (vs 30).

We have seen past theological movements that attempted to build the *ekklesia* based upon authority and submission. It created a culture of law, legalism and forced relationships with leaders. The Father Movement introduced authority by building a culture of honor based upon a covenantal heart.

Jesus started His ministry by entering His hometown of Nazareth. We read in Mark 6 that their response to Christ's ministry was one of *dishonor* (vs 4) and *unbelief* (vs 6). Dishonor and unbelief undermined the anointing: *"He was not able to do even one work of power there, except He laid His Hands on a few sickly people and healed them"* (vs 5). A spirit of dishonor shuts the door to the operation of the supernatural and kingdom advancement.

What would happen in the *ekklesia* if *"who do you think that you are"* was replaced with *"blessed is he that comes in the name of the Lord?"* It takes an enduring commitment by all to overthrow the *'culture of dishonor'* and replace it with the *'kingdom spirit of honor.'* It takes a willingness to wage spiritual warfare against this enemy as it does not leave the premises without a fight.

When leaders function honorably, when sons and daughters bestow the gift of honor on the Lord, His Word, the operation of the Spirit, God's leaders, the older in our midst, and so on, anything is possible. When the *ekklesia* is caught up with honoring each other above themselves, forming a spiritual honor guard, there is hope for the 21st Century Church to change the world.

A Covenantal Commitment Must Be Active Towards Each Other

God is a God of covenant, keeping His covenant to a thousand generations. The *ekklesia* are a covenantal people, united by their recognition of the New Covenant in His blood. Covenant recognizes that if one suffers, all suffer, and if one is honoured, all are honoured (1 Cor 12:26). It practices living out the Word within community (Greek koinonia), ensuring true family and fellowship. It embraces and loves brothers and sisters with Christ's passion.

As the Godhead covenanted with each other and entered the dance, so too does the *ekklesia*.

The picture that comes to me in terms of what this practically looks like is found in Joel's depiction of the *"army"* of God: ***"They run like warriors. They climb the wall like soldiers. They each march [straight ahead] in line, and they do not deviate from their paths. They do not crowd each other; each one marches in his path. When they burst through the defenses (weapons), they do not break ranks.... The Lord utters His voice before His army, for His camp is very great, because strong and powerful is he who [obediently] carries out His word"*** (2:6-7, 11).

I have a precious friend. When we talk together of things that are happening in our nation and we conclude what we sense must be said or done, he ends our time together by saying, *"I got your six!"* The saying has its origin with WWII American fighter pilots. It meant: *"I've got your back"* or, *"I'm watching your blindside."*

Even when Christ felt abandoned and forsaken on the cross, He was not. The Father had His back and would not let Him go down into Sheol without a back-up plan. That back-up plan was because of the covenant: the Heavenly Father manifested that covenantal commitment with resurrection power.

A Commitment To Love Unconditionally

Love is the highest form of obedience. Jesus said, *"**If you really love Me, you will keep and obey My commandments**"* (Jn 14:15). Love is a choice and not just a feeling, a decision to love one another as He loved us (Jn 13:34). It is non-optional.

The God who inspired 1 Corinthians 13 lives this out Himself. God never asks us to do something we are incapable of doing. His Spirit works within us to both will and do what please Him. Practicing loving on one another as He loved on us is critical to the *ekklesia* success.

The Message translation of 1 Corinthians 13:4-7 provides a very clear road with guardrails: God's agape love…

"cares more for others than for self.
doesn't want what it doesn't have.
doesn't strut,
doesn't have a swelled head,
doesn't force itself on others,
isn't always "me first,"
doesn't fly off the handle,
doesn't keep score of the sins of others,
doesn't revel when others grovel,
takes pleasure in the flowering of truth,

David Kalamen

puts up with anything,
trusts God always,
always looks for the best,
never looks back but keeps going to
the end."

"God's love never sees limits but always seeks outlets, and it is never diminished by giving it away." Christ's expectation of the character of a Christian was seen through this grid: **"By this everyone will know that you are My disciples, if you have love and unselfish concern for one another"** (Jn 13:35).

The *"one another"* scriptures are an outflow of this primary command to **"love one another."** It is almost impossible for us to forgive one another, be gracious towards one another, encourage one another, pray for one another, be devoted towards one another, build up one another, carry one another's burdens, bear with one another, speak the truth to one another, and live in peace with one another – if we do not love one another.

Paul wrote: **"Make my joy complete by being of the same mind, having the same love [toward one another], knit together in spirit, intent on one purpose [and living a life that reflects your faith and spreads the gospel...]"** (Phil 2:2). Where do we get that **"same love"** but from the same Source, the Holy Spirit.

I add my prayer to the apostle Paul's prayer for the *ekklesia*: ***"May you, having been [deeply] rooted and [securely] grounded in love, be fully capable of comprehending with all the saints (God's people) the width and length and height and depth of His love [fully experiencing that amazing, endless love]; and [that you may come] to know [practically, through personal experience] the love of Christ which far surpasses [mere] knowledge [without experience], that you may be filled up [throughout your being] to all the fullness of God [so that you may have the richest experience of God's presence in your lives, completely filled and flooded with God Himself]"*** (Eph 3:17-19).

We have the capacity to give away what we have been given. The world's introduction to the *ekklesia* should be a counter-cultural experience with what heaven should look like. The ***"God who so loved the world"*** (Jn 3:16) should be loving that world through His Church. That love should be practiced in the household of faith, first, so that the world can see how we love one another.

David Kalamen

A Commitment To Integrity

The *ekklesia* is all about walking and living in integrity. Both leaders and the spiritual family are called upon to be trustworthy. Who we are must be consistently in line with what it means to be **"recreated in His image"** (Eph 2:10), acknowledging that we are His workmanship and reflect His work.

Our words must carry integrity, meaning what we say and saying what we mean. Our actions, and the way we conduct ourselves, must be accountable. Our plans must be ethical. Our intentions and agenda must be godly. The way we do business must be upfront and honest. Our bills are paid on time.

Integrity is an overflow towards people of the way we conduct ourselves with the Lord. If we are honest in our relationship with God, it will overflow in our relationship with each other. If we value and honour God's Word, our words will take on the same value towards others. When the *ekklesia* is uncompromising regarding developing a culture of integrity, the world will take notice.

Integrity is driven by ethical principles: it is the opposite of hypocrisy. If God said it, we believe it, and that settles it. There is nothing more beautiful than when the *ekklesia* chooses holiness over temptation and compromise. Holy people carry the heart of Joseph: *"How can I do this great evil and sin against God?"* (Gen 39:9, AMP). The Bible says, *"He who walks in integrity and with moral character walks securely..."* (Pr 10:9).

Maintaining integrity of the heart is a big deal. God *"tests the heart and delights in uprightness and integrity"* (1 Chron 29:17). *"God will not reject a man of integrity"* (Job 8:20). Functioning with integrity is our only hope of divine intervention and salvation. God is not forced to rescue those who function deceitfully, and neither will He intervene for the *ekklesia* to bail out its iniquity. Sin will be dealt with first, then integrity must be restored to see blessing.

David asks and answers his own question: *"Who may dwell [continually] on Your holy hill? He who walks with integrity and strength of character, and works righteousness, and speaks and holds truth in his heart"* (Ps 15:1-2). *"The eyes of the Lord are toward the righteous [those with moral courage and spiritual integrity] and His ears are open to their cry"* (Ps 34:15).

When integrity is lost, everything is lost: *"Like a muddied fountain and a polluted spring is a righteous man who yields and compromises his integrity..."* (Pr 25:26). Who wants to drink from a muddied fountain or a polluted spring? God is looking for a pure heart and an uncompromised soul. The *ekklesia* is called to a higher standard than the world, for we live our lives before an audience of One and He will eventually judge everything said and done.

A Commitment To Letting His Word Rule

Either the world will rule the *ekklesia* or the Word of God will rule. When Jesus was assaulted by the enemy in the wilderness, He let the Word of God defend Him. Our only defense is the authenticity, authority and efficacy of His Word. Second Timothy 3:15-17 (Msg) says:

"There's nothing like the written Word of God for showing you the way to salvation through faith in Christ Jesus. Every part of Scripture is God-breathed and useful one way or another—showing us truth, exposing our rebellion, correcting our mistakes, training us to live God's way. Through the Word we are put

together and shaped up for the tasks God has for us."

It is often challenging when we encounter people who believe that quoting scripture is tantamount to legalism. The Word of God is the final arbiter of truth, the standard by which every conflict is resolved, and the only authority that can define whether resolve is healthy or not. It is alive and works to divide between carnal and spiritual motivations.

Don't allow the Word of God to be dismissed or disrespected. Remember, the Word of God was so important that it is personified in Christ Himself. He is the Word of God. ***"In the beginning [before all time] was the Word (Christ), and the Word was with God, and the Word was God Himself. He was [continually existing] in the beginning [co-eternally] with God"*** (Jn 1:1-2).

Allow His Word to rule our hearts and minds, not opinions, philosophies, and theories. Let His Word settle all matters regarding faith and function. We have seen the incredible damage that occurs to the church when men's words and opinions overrule God's Word, when the world's opinion of what the church should be outweighs God's opinion of what His *ekklesia* should be.

These relational and governmental values constitute a vital plumb line for the emergence of what I call an *'apostolic governance'* model for the *ekklesia*. It is my belief that it provides the organic structure for how the 21st Century church should function. There is no question in my mind that if these values are yielded to as the primary building code, the modern church can survive and thrive. If we surrender to His thoughts and ways, ultimately, we will see His paths, His message, His ministers, and His methodologies emerge that will make His *ekklesia* relevant and successful.

This model is going to require brutal honesty from church leaders. It is clear to me that any breach of these fundamental values places the present church at risk of self-destructing. We have seen too many one-generational success stories followed by a quick descent into chaos with either moral or governmental corruption.

There is no guarantee of success. However, there is absolutely no opportunity for success if we disregard or violate these essential values. Grafting these values into our governance model will create a guide as to how leaders should function and engage in the business of the *ekklesia*.

We need to follow Christ's example. The *ekklesia* He is building is intended to represent the heart of His Father in every way. What we build with His permission and the way we build it should also be done with the desire to honor the Father. Remember, it is His House, not ours. He has the final word on how His family functions and what is projected to the world.

Chapter 12
Repairing Foundational Cracks In Present Church Governance

"For these seven rejoice to see the plumb line in the hand of Zerubbabel. They are the eyes of the Lord, which scan to and fro throughout the whole earth."
Zechariah 4:10 (NKJV)

Any builder knows the importance of a plumb line. A plumb line is also called a plummet, a string with a non-magnetic weight connected to one end. When the line is held so that the weight can fall freely, an exact vertical measurement can be defined. Painters and carpenters use plumb lines to make precise vertical lines for their work.

A plumb line utilizes the law of gravity to discover proper angles, reveal the most direct and true path from top to bottom, keep things plumb, or level. A plumb line doesn't alter or shift with the will and impulses of the carpenter. It remains true, and all work must line up with it. Gravity controls the natural plummet, but scripture reveals that it is His eyes that control the spiritual plummet.

In this section it is vital that we use the governance style of the Godhead as a plumb line to evaluate the modern church. In the way that Jesus cleansed the Temple, the Father's House, the Holy Spirit needs to clean house today, sweeping away every manmade tradition and religious philosophy that does not align itself to true north.

Jesus reminded us that if we hear the Word of God and do not build accordingly, what will be built will surely be vulnerable to the *"until factors."* If our governmental structures and methodologies are not in alignment to His Word, God cannot protect the *ekklesia* from failure and ultimate diminishment.

In this section it is my intention to challenge present day church government practice in several areas that have been commonly grafted into denominational or local church policy and protocol. You can discern for yourselves whether this accurately describes a potential danger or not.

I am aware that changing local church governance is not an easy process. If the emergence of the *ekklesia* is as important as I believe it is, I know there will be a spiritual battle for control. It may involve ideology, opinions, personalities, politics, and so on, but the battle for righteousness must be won.

We are living in a day when to question the status quo of how the church governs itself is threatening. Many beliefs and systems are so ingrained that it would take a significant amount of time to acknowledge wrong and reverse course. Most people, including pastors, are resistant to change. So, this may be an uphill battle, even if one would desire to shift the culture.

I understand and I realise that I have had the rare opportunity to initiate this form of governance from the inception of Kelowna Christian Center. Our spiritual family have been trained and equipped in this way of seeing the Church as the *ekklesia*. Still, the vision bucket has holes in it, and our covenantal membership process of adding people to the church takes great effort to educate those who are new to this form of governance.

Thankfully, I have seen many heads nod in affirmation of our governance model as they see the wisdom and practicality in its expression. So, let's address the following.

David Kalamen

The Tradition Of Preaching For A Call

A quick search on Google will review numerous articles that will mentor pastors preaching for a call to lead a church. This is a common process as a congregation is given the opportunity to evaluate a pastor's readiness and ability to lead a church. Often, they are recommended to a church board, a Sunday is chosen for them to preach, and a time is set for a vote on their viability.

This process can become quite political and messy, as pastors and their families come under a microscope. It has at times been very hurtful when the voting process establishes acceptance or rejection and by what percentage or margin of votes. The democratic process has displaced the theocratic process.

There are numerous observations or concerns with this process from my perspective. I pose questions and make observations that deserve spiritual reflection, insights that need to be tested by the light of God's Word.

1. Are churches in this situation because they have not developed sons and daughters that they can transition leadership to? They may have associate and assistant pastors,

but do they have sons and daughters trained in the DNA of the house, who know the people, the history and purpose for which the church was birthed?

2. The Bible exhorts us to **"*know those who labor among you*"** (1 Thess 5:12) – does one Sunday morning preach accomplish that goal? Much thought would have to be given to the recommendation of the interviewing committee.
3. Is the interviewing committee, in charge of recommendations, spiritually mature enough to do so? Are they elders or business leaders? What qualifications do they have to discern spiritual leadership?
4. What percentage of the vote is required for a pastor or congregation to feel that this is a good decision, knowing that any percentage brings into play both an acceptance and rejection ratio?
5. Who calls a new leader of the local church? Is it the Board, the congregation, or the Lord? If the Lord is the One who is doing the calling, then the role of the congregation is affirmation, not election.
6. Does this process politicize the church into for and against camps?
7. Does this process tend to create

> ***"hirelings"*** versus ***"shepherds"*** (Jn 10:12-13), those who will run when the wolves – i.e. demonic opposition, personality conflicts, doctrinal error - threaten the flock of God versus those who will lay down their lives and fight for the life of the *ekklesia*?

I remember processing a situation with a young pastor who was being asked to *"lay down his life for the flock and leave for the good of the church."* I challenged his heart: the way a true shepherd lays down his life is by staying and defending the flock. What he was facing needed spiritual leadership and leadership that was prepared to risk his reputation to uphold the Lord's.

All of this is said with the recognition that *'good leaders'* have been chosen to oversee God's house by local congregations. The challenge of my heart is that we do not devolve into Israel's motivation in choosing Saul to lead them so that they would have a king like the nations around them (1 Sam 8:5). Though I truly believe that God did not set Israel or Saul up for failure (1 Sam 8:17), God had His own choice in the wings and their drive for a king took them on a tragic journey.

The Role Of The Apostolic In The Local Church

When one looks at the Book of Acts – what Irenaeous called *The Acts of the Apostles* - we see the word apostle used thirty-one times. The term pastor is referred to but once in the entire New Testament (Eph 4:11). Some theologians explain that the early Church was growing and expanding and needed apostolic doctrine and leadership. I can understand that.

However, does not the 21st Century Church need growth and expansion as well? There is still a large percentage of the world's population that have yet to encounter the *ekklesia*. Jesus is the Chief Cornerstone: the apostles and prophets are referred to as foundational (Eph 2:20). I would then say that every local church needs an apostolic influence to establish strong foundations.

The modern denominational model has become more pastoral in nature and has relegated the apostolic function to missionary activity. The apostolic calling and gifting is clearly related to being a *"sent one, a messenger, like an ambassador or envoy representing another kingdom."* However, it is much more than that.

The apostolic gift is one of the five-fold gifts spoken of in Ephesians 4:11-16, a representation of the Person and ministry of Christ, *"**the Apostle of our faith**,"* to His Church (Heb 3:1).

- They carry authority to train doctrinally, raise up, build, and bless (Acts 2:42; 2 Cor 10:8)
- Their commission had to do with a specific people, place, or scope of authority (2 Cor 10:13-18)
- They set into order new works (1 Cor 12:28; Tit 1:5)
- They carry a burden for the whole of the churches under their care (2 Cor 11:28)
- They function out of their calling and relationship to spiritual sons and daughters, leadership teams and churches, by birth or adoption, and do so through voluntary recognition and honor

It has been said that *"every pastor needs a pastor."* The question then lies in *"who is pastoring the pastor?"* Every pastor in authority needs to be under authority. I have found that when pastors pastor pastors, the *ekklesia* is in management mode. When apostolic leaders pastor pastors, they move pastors to grow personally and expand the *ekklesia's* sphere of spiritual influence.

Our Bible Colleges excel in training pastors, teachers, worship leaders, Christian educators, and so on, but where is the training of apostolic callings, giftings and anointings? From my experience, apostles father sons and daughters who become apostles in their own right. It is caught, not just taught. It is the Paul/Timothy dynamic and that is vitally needed for success in present church systems.

My intention is not to diminish the role of the pastor locally, but to raise up the role of the apostolic. Scripture says when Christ ascended, He gave apostles as a gift to the Church (Eph 4:11). Paul wrote that *"God has set some in the church, first apostles, secondarily prophets, thirdly teachers, and after that, miracles, then gifts of healings, helps, governments, diversities of tongues..."* (1 Cor 12:28, KJV).

The order was definitive: *"first apostles, secondarily prophets..."* The Church needed solid doctrinal foundations and moral character. God's people needed solid spiritual foundations and personal and corporate integrity. The Word and the Spirit have always built together, as I have already alluded to in this document.

So....

- Does the pastor need apostolic fathering?
- Does the local church need apostolic influence and input?
- Does the 21st Century church see their need?

The issue is not authority and control: the real issue is fathering and influence. If the pastor or the church has an apostolic leader in their life, they should be drawn upon and valued. Paul was not after control, but to use his God-given calling and anointing to strengthen God's leaders and the Church.

He wrote the Corinthian church: ***"For even if you were to have ten thousand teachers [to guide you] in Christ, yet you would not have many fathers [who led you to Christ and assumed responsibility for you], for I became your father in Christ Jesus through the good news [of salvation]....So I urge you, be imitators of me [just as a child imitates his father]"*** (1 Cor 4:15-16).

He felt he had the right to speak into their lives, whether they accepted or rejected that counsel, because he had ***"become"*** their father in Christ through receiving the Gospel. In 2 Corinthians 10:13, he says, ***"We, on the other hand, will not boast beyond our proper limit, but [will keep] within the limits of our commission (territory, authority) which God has granted to us as a measure, which reaches and includes even you."*** He speaks of them as his beloved children whom he can come to with a rod of correction, or in a spirit of love.

Pastors Committed To Long Term 'Spiritual Fathering

For a pastor to pastor with the heart of the Heavenly Father, they need a revelation of the Father and of the apostolic call to father. Scripture is clear on the pastoral call and function: Ezekiel 34 wraps up the call in five very vital words - feed, heal and strengthen, restore, rule, and protect the flock of God. While the apostolic gift may carry oversight over a number of churches, the pastoral gift is called to be planted and remain.

Let me make a special note before continuing. When I use the phrase, *'spiritual fathering,'* it is not used to express that our spiritual birth emerged from a person. Scripture is clear in John 1:12-13:

> *"But to as many as did receive and welcome Him, He gave the right [the authority, the privilege] to become children of God, that is, to those who believe in (adhere to, trust in, and rely on) His name—who were born, not of blood [natural conception], nor of the will of the flesh [physical impulse], nor of the will of man [that of a natural father], but of God [that is, a divine and supernatural birth—*

they are born of God—spiritually transformed, renewed, sanctified]."

Clearly, no man can be your *'spiritual father'* in that sense other than God Himself. It is His Spirit who gives you life. It is His Word that acts as a force that brings about spiritual conception: *"You have been born again [that is, reborn from above—spiritually transformed, renewed, and set apart for His purpose] not of seed which is perishable but from that which is imperishable and immortal, that is, through the living and everlasting word of God"* (1 Pet 1:23).

Jesus spoke of this as being *"born again"* (Jn 3:6-7 - *"That which is born of the flesh is flesh [the physical is merely physical], and that which is born of the Spirit is spirit. Do not be surprised that I have told you, 'You must be born again [reborn from above—spiritually transformed, renewed, sanctified]'"*).

However, what is needed is *fathers (and mothers) in the faith.* John spoke of the difference between babes who have had their sins forgiven and are coming to know God, young men who have battled spiritual forces, and fathers who know Him who existed before the beginning (1 Jn 2:13-14).

His Church, His Way

If we are going to see the *ekklesia* reach its potential, pastors need to be connected to apostolic leaders. They need to carry a long-term commitment to raise a spiritual family. They can make disciples, mentor the next generation, coach assistants in spiritual life skills, but are they committed to raise sons and daughters?

Raising sons and daughters will take a significantly longer time than what most pastors are willing to spend. It may take a lifetime commitment to *"grow old"* together and be in each other's lives but what great joy occurs when sons and daughters are positioned to take their place and carry on building the *ekklesia*. Remember, there is little to no success without a successor.

So, some questions need to be addressed:

- Is the local church willing to take a pastor on indefinitely with the intended purpose of building a spiritual family and growing a sphere of spiritual influence?
- Is the pastor willing to give his life for a spiritual family and commit to developing a long-term influence?
- Are sons and daughters recognizable and ready to take up the baton of leadership, to continue enlarging on what has already been established?
- Is there a process in place?

- Has the heart of the Father been taught, and has the spirit of sonship been caught?

Well, what if the pastor is not the right fit? Then that question needs to be resolved by the apostolic authority. Sometimes pastors need personal help, doctrinal correction, and restorative counsel. Sometimes church congregations need the same. Like any family, there are no perfect leaders or churches. However, imperfections do not necessarily disqualify anyone or any church. Sometimes the imperfections you know are easier to deal with than the imperfections in someone you do not know that you want to bring in to take their place.

Appointed Versus Elected Leaders

In many local church governance models new leaders who are willing to serve are located and evaluated by a nominating committee, then placed before a congregation for a vote. This stands in significant contrast to Paul's direction to his **"true child in common faith,"** Titus (1:4), to **"set right what remains unfinished, and appoint elders in every city as I directed you"** (vs 5).

The early disciples, in their desire to replace Judas, *"cast lots"* between Justus and Matthias, and it fell on Matthias (Acts 1:23-26). Church history remains relatively silent on what became of Matthias, or his ministry.

However, God had his man, Saul of Damascus, and Paul's entire apostolic ministry was challenged continuously because it didn't fit the traditional way. It took years for the Church apostolic leadership to acknowledge and recognize that Paul was the one selected, appointed and anointed by God. Unfortunately, the *electoral process* has often led to a politicization of the Church and to the emergence of cliques (1 Cor 1:12).

I have witnessed the politicization of the church governance process. For example, say seven leaders are selected by a nominating committee to replace three board members who are stepping down. We have all seen the politicking that can go on in the foyer as each leader seeks votes to ensure their election.

The resolution comes when three with the most votes are elected and four are rejected. The consequences are myriad as to what occurs in the ego of men and women who did not make the grade. Those who got behind their man or woman often carry an entitlement to have their opinions listened to and valued. Those elected often feel that they are on the Board representing their constituency to the pastor, rather than representing the Lord and their pastor to the congregation.

In most situations elected Board members realise that the pastor is transitory, but the people will remain. The power base is with the people, not with the pastor who comes and goes every 3.6 years on average. Elected leaders see themselves as being put in place by their peers, accountable to their peers.

What would happen if the election process was displaced by the appointment process, an apostolic model? What if we drew upon the wisdom and discernment of the apostolic in choosing men and women to serve? Paul counselled Titus (1:6-9) as to the quality of the person who would represent Heavenly Father in His House:

"A man of unquestionable integrity, the husband of one wife, having children who believe, not accused of being immoral or rebellious. For the overseer, as God's steward, must be blameless, not self-willed, not quick-tempered, not addicted to wine, not violent, not greedy for dishonest gain [but financially ethical]. He must be hospitable [to believers, as well as

strangers], a lover of what is good, sensible (upright), fair, devout, self-disciplined [above reproach— whether in public or in private]. He must hold firmly to the trustworthy word [of God] as it was taught to him, so that he will be able both to give accurate instruction in sound [reliable, error-free] doctrine and to refute those who contradict [it by explaining their error]."

What if three people were discerned and appointed by spiritual oversight for three positions? What if each stood before the congregation for affirmation alone, and on their own merits? What would happen if both the leadership and congregation agreed to their appointment? What strength would that bring to the sense of being placed by the Lord into that role?

The *ekklesia* is not a religious or corporate structure: it is the Father's House. When we come into His House, His house rules must be affirmed and our thinking must be aligned to the fact that He is doing a new thing. We need to discern this *'new thing'* and be willing to make the changes necessary.

David Kalamen

Unanimity Versus Majority Vote

I have already addressed the vital importance of unified leadership and action. It is one of the greatest expressions of the government of God and is demonstrated in the relationships that exist in the Godhead. The early Church pursued unity as a priority. It was the Holy Spirit who guided the process, making the will and mind of God clear.

Listen to the counsel of the Spirit manifesting in Paul's exhortation to the Ephesians:

"So I, the prisoner for the Lord, appeal to you to live a life worthy of the calling to which you have been called [that is, to live a life that exhibits godly character, moral courage, personal integrity, and mature behavior—a life that expresses gratitude to God for your salvation], with all humility [forsaking self-righteousness], and gentleness [maintaining self-control], with patience, bearing with one another in [unselfish] love. Make every effort to keep the oneness of the Spirit in the bond of peace [each individual working together to make

the whole successful]. There is one body [of believers] and one Spirit— just as you were called to one hope when called [to salvation]—one Lord, one faith, one baptism, one God and Father of us all who is [sovereign] over all and [working] through all and [living] in all" (4:1-5).

I like the Message translation of verse 4: *"You were all called to travel on the same road and in the same direction, so stay together, both outwardly and inwardly."* That is very difficult for many strong men and women, used to leading in their sphere of life, to yield to. It takes humility, courage, and maturity to do so without pushing a personal agenda.

Much of the 21st Century church governmental system aligns itself to a corporate model of *'majority voting power'* rather than aligning itself to a kingdom model of *'authority through unity.'* I have heard many reactions to this re-alignment: let me address a few.

- *"It is anti-democratic."* Wikipedia defines democracy (from Ancient Greek: δημοκρατία, romanized: dēmokratía, dēmo*s 'people'* and kratos *'rule'*) as *"a system of government in which state power is vested in the* *people or the general population of a state…and rulers are elected through competitive elections."*

We have already addressed the inherent dangers within the elective versus appointment process and the ecclesiastical systems need to be de-politicalized and yield to higher thoughts and ways.

- *"It is anti-personal rights."* When we came to Christ and surrendered to His Lordship, we lost personal rights to our own way of thinking, our own way of feeling, our own way of acting, and our own way of speaking. Our opinions are now subject to His. This is His Church, His House, the *ekklesia*, and He has full rights. Our role is to think His thoughts, feel His heart, act in accordance with His character, and speak in a way that honours Him.

- *"It is forcing group think."* Well, unanimity is not a forced thing: it is a voluntary thing. It is not a matter of convenience as much as a matter of conviction. Strong leaders can have strong opinions, but their leadership strength is not found in their opinions but in their capacity to submit to God's thinking over their own.

Each leader must be given the freedom to speak what they discern, and this needs to be respected. However, each leader must prayerfully come to the table having spent time with God on matters so that they come to the place that the apostles did in Antioch: ***"It seems good to us and the Holy Spirit"*** (Acts 15:28). This matures leaders and holds them accountable to hear the voice of the Lord amid all the noise.

- *It produces 'yes' men and women.* Yes, it does. It is better than *'no'* men and women. I love to hear the *'yes'* and *'amen'* from the Lord to His promises, and I am grateful when those walking with me strive for agreement. Their *'yes'* must be to God, His will, and His Word. Their strength lies in their capacity to see what saying *'yes'* to God will accomplish. The Acts of the Apostles written about in the Book of Acts clearly manifest unity, agreeing, saying *'yes'* to God and His Word, as a priority of kingdom living. They had their disputes but settled them together in unity.

- *It requires leaders who subordinate their true feelings, kowtow to peer pressure, or violate their conscience.* Hopefully, that is not the case. Leaders are chosen because they know God. John addressed the babes because their sins were forgiven, the young men because they had victory over the devil, but fathers because they knew God (1 Jn 2:13-14). If leaders capitulate on their conscientious convictions to the *'crowd,'* there is a leadership deficit. We do not make decisions on feelings, opinions, peer pressure, or conscience, but by the leading of the Holy Spirit and the confirmation of His Word. It requires placing leaders who know God in positions of decision-making.

There is much authority that flows from the *principle of agreement.* In Matthew 18:19, Jesus said: **"If two believers on earth agree [that is, are of one mind, in harmony] about anything that they ask [within the will of God], it will be done for them by My Father in heaven"** (AMP). Jesus said, **"I love the Father, I do exactly as the Father has commanded Me [and act in full agreement with Him]"** (Jn 14:31).

Did that mean that Christ lost His identity and personal rights by yielding to His Father? No! Did that mean that He was less than His Father by doing so? No! Neither do we lose personhood or freedom by looking for the will of God, listening to His voice, and acting on His directions for the *ekklesia*.

Amos said, **"Can two walk together, except they be agreed?"** (3:3, KJV). If leaders cannot get into agreement, how can they lead, less walk together? The counsel of Paul was this: **"I urge you, believers, by the name of our Lord Jesus Christ, that all of you be in full agreement in what you say, and that there be no divisions or factions among you, but that you be perfectly united in your way of thinking and in your judgment [about matters of the faith]"** (1 Cor 1:10).

What happens when we are not in agreement? From my perspective, the decision leadership is discussing is not the priority over the need to be in unity with the Lord and each other. In our apostolic governance model, we have delayed decisions to give time for prayer. In three occasions over forty-two years of leadership, I saw the Lord turn everyone's hearts from a *'split board'* to a unified one at critical points of decision making. I trust the Holy Spirit.

It cannot be *'my way or the highway.'* Our personal egos and agendas must be left at the door. God is not so much interested in your thoughts as He is in whether you will yield to reason: **"Come, let us reason together"** (Isa 1:18, KJV). The benefit of the power of agreement so outweighs getting our personal opinions aired.

In our apostolic structure, our striving for unity together as a board or, as I sometimes refer to it, an apostolic team, levels the playing field. The apostolic leader is required to lead, but yield decision-making to the process of agreement. This forces everyone around the table to seek God, both leader and Board, so that kingdom initiatives can advance.

We have written this principle into our operating strategy:

> *"It is critical that the leadership continue to affirm, legally and functionally, the "principle of unanimity" as the working principle for board action, meaning that – each board member, in order to assure heart agreement and unanimity in the decision process, would have to have the following issues satisfied: that being said, decisions did not –*
>
> - *compromise Bible standards of morality*
> - *seriously jeopardize the financial stability of the organization*
> - *undermine any fundamental doctrine outlined in*

the statement of faith
- *violate Biblical standards of integrity in doing business*
- *circumvent established lines of authority established within its governance structure, or*
- *place a serious threat to the unity of the Body of Christ, internally or within the context of the city."*

In my experience as a leader, while counselling churches who are facing the *"until factor"* of difficulty, I have seen the devastating effects of *'majority vote power.'* We all know that majority rule is not always righteous rule. The will of God is not found in numbers, but in His Word.

The Bible says that ***"a house divided against itself cannot stand"*** (Matt 12:25, KJV). Division occurs because of *'di-vision'*, two competing visions and double-mindedness in the leadership. James warns the *ekklesia*:

"If any of you lacks wisdom [to guide him through a decision or circumstance], he is to ask of [our benevolent] God, who gives to everyone generously and without rebuke or blame, and it will be given to him. But he must ask [for wisdom] in faith, without doubting [God's willingness to help], for the one who doubts is like a billowing surge of the

sea that is blown about and tossed by the wind. For such a person ought not to think or expect that he will receive anything [at all] from the Lord, being a double-minded man, unstable and restless in all his ways [in everything he thinks, feels, or decides]" (1:5-8).

Did you hear that? Do not think or expect that he will receive anything at all from the Lord. Judas got into trouble when he pursued his vision for Christ's life other than the Father's will (Matt 27:3). Saul got into trouble because he wanted the people's approval more that God's (1 Sam 13:11).

Paul stated in Galatians 1:10: **"Am I now trying to win the favor and approval of men, or of God? Or am I seeking to please someone? If I were still trying to be popular with men, I would not be a bondservant of Christ."**

Humanity got the attention of God in Genesis 11 as the **"whole earth spoke one language and used the same vocabulary"** (vs 1). They said, **"Come, let us build a city for ourselves...."** (vs 4). God heard it and came down to see what they were doing. What He then said is profound: **"Behold, they are one [unified] people, and they all have the same language. This is only the beginning** *of what they will do [in rebellion against Me], and now no evil thing they imagine they can do will be impossible for them"* (vs 6).

In this instance, it was unity used against God's will, building for themselves and not for the Lord. What could happen through the *ekklesia* if we all spoke the same language, used the same vocabulary, and built His House, His way, together? The response of heaven would be equally profound: *"No good thing they imagine they can do will be impossible for them."*

Term Limits?

I know that both Society Act input and corporate best practice counsel for term limits on members of the Board. In some situations, one is not given a choice. The question is whether this is Biblical, or even sound counsel. It has been my experience that term limits do more damage than good.

When does an elder cease becoming an elder? When does a father stop being a father? I have found that there is immense value in serving in leadership together for the long haul. The relational equity that is built together is invaluable. Like a husband and wife who have been together for awhile, the longer they have spent time praying and communicating together, the more they know and trust how each other believes, thinks and decides.

I know transitions need to occur, that leaders leave, retire, move away, or pass on, circumstances change, vocations shift, demands on the family require resignation, moral failure demands removal, and so on. Disqualification is a very real risk. It was Paul's greatest concern as he stated in 1 Corinthians 9:25-27:

> *"Now every athlete who [goes into training and] competes in the games is disciplined and exercises self-control in all things. They do it to win a crown that withers, but we [do it to receive] an imperishable [crown that cannot wither]. Therefore I do not run without a definite goal; I do not flail around like one beating the air [just shadow boxing]. But [like a boxer] I strictly discipline my body and make it my slave, so that, after I have preached [the gospel] to others, I myself will not somehow be disqualified [as unfit for service]".*

However, I have been thrilled to see literally hundreds of years of leadership equity occur at the KCCS Board level among faithful, God-fearing leaders. We can look back together at what the Lord has done, why He did it, and remember the process that was used to make the decisions we did. There is history, and there is an accumulation and wealth of wisdom. That is lost through forced term limits.

Well, people might ask: *"Is that not undermining creativity, the injection of new blood, or the integration of next generational influence?"* I have found that all these questions can be answered in broadening the input into the Board's decision-making process by adding new Board members strategically, and by opening access to the Board to next generational leaders through non-voting membership options and reporting venues.

The old and young need to work together. We need to see the wisdom of the aged alongside the vitality and creative vision of the younger. Both the old paths and the new paths need to be laid out with understanding (Matt 13:52). The kingdom of God is built on the scribe and disciple studying and working together. The House of God is built and filled with the antique and modern furniture together. This is the calling on spiritual leadership, to know the power of the right combination.

Votes Of Confidence

This option has been used by many *'members'* in congregational meetings, espousing their right to have a vote on whether leadership should remain or be replaced. Unfortunately, the vote of confidence has often turned into a vote of non-confidence. I have watched this process as the son of a pastor during annual congregational meetings, knowing that the wrong vote meant my dad was out of a job and we would be moving on as a family. I have witnessed pastors' struggles with the vote: *"What percentage did they need to remain in place, knowing that a certain percentage felt that their time was over?"*

When an individual is caught in a sin, the Bible says, **"you who are spiritual [that is, you who are responsive to the guidance of the Spirit] are to restore such a person in a spirit of gentleness [not with a sense of superiority or self-righteousness], keeping a watchful eye on yourself, so that you are not tempted as well"** (Gal 6:1).

What happens when a leader needs discipline, correction, or adjustment? Paul counselled the Church in 1 Tim 5:17-20:

> **"The elders who perform their leadership duties well are to be considered worthy of double honor (financial support), especially those who work hard at preaching and teaching [the word of God concerning eternal salvation through Christ]. For the Scripture says, "You shall not muzzle the ox while it is treading out**

the grain [to keep it from eating]," and, "The worker is worthy of his wages [he deserves fair compensation]." Do not accept an accusation against an elder unless it is based on [the testimony of at least] two or three witnesses. As for those [elders] who continue in sin, reprimand them in the presence of all [the congregation], so that the rest will be warned."

As honor needs to be doubled for those who do their job well, so warning needs to be doubled for those who do not.

If an individual requires the involvement of the spiritually mature, leaders require the involvement of the spiritually mature. Pastors need an apostle or an apostolic team that they are willing to submit to. I am grateful for pastors and apostolic leaders in my life, men and women who I have relational equity with, who know my life and character, who have access to my wife and children, and who can be brought in by the leadership to address any area of my life.

I can be removed from office by the majority of the membership, by the unanimous will of the Board, or by the counsel of an apostolic team I am submitted to who serve the Board. I did not set myself into leadership. I serve by the call of God. I am not in the ministry: the ministry is in me. Even if I am unrighteously removed, God will raise me up and the call and ministry will continue. There is nothing to fear in true accountability: it is one of the highest forms of freedom.

However, my confidence is not in man's affirmation of my calling, though living with a clean and clear reputation with God and man is important. My confidence is in the Lord and His calling, His appointment to service, and in the anointing.

Serving alongside men and women who know me, and have watched my life, has been an honour. I trust them, and I trust God in them. Serving the spiritual family God has graced me with has been one of the greatest joys of my life. Seeing sons and daughters carrying the torch into another generation, enlarging their sphere of spiritual influence, gives me hope for the Church, His *ekklesia*.

We have precious little time to repair these cracks in the foundation and walls of the modern church. Time is of the essence. Leaders need to return to building His Church, the ekklesia, His way. They need to see the present necessity of changing course and rebuilding what in many ways has been broken due to religious tradition, the import of corporate structural ideas, and to yielding to government control.

Chapter 13
The Necessity And Joy In Transition

"Spiritual fathers understand that true success requires humbly passing the baton to faithful sons and daughters."

When Kelowna Christian Center Society was established in 1982, God gave me this word for our leadership team: ***"Who [with reason] despises the day of small things (beginnings)"*** (Zech 4:10)? Little did I know that within forty-two years we would have trained many leaders for the ministry, planted numerous churches, reached out in missions to 35+ nations, created significant technology and curriculum streams, and become a leader in Christian education, both through blended and online forums.

Who could have thought that what started with one pastor commissioned to multi-task - preach, counsel, do accounting, visit, administrate, clean, sweep and set up chairs, and so on – would, forty-two years later, see close to one thousand staff working together to facilitate the vision? One can never underestimate a God-thought, like the smallest mustard seed planted in the ground, whose leaves cast an incredible reach.

As leaders began to recognize the growth, both spiritually and organizationally, they would ask me: *"What is your five-year plan?"* Honestly, my plans emerged from prayer, and often times, the Father was answering my requests just in time for next steps. I was not as much *'purpose-driven'* as I was *'presence-driven.'* I needed to hear His voice and feel His Hand before I could pursue His plan.

However, as the apostolic began to grow in me, God gave me my answer. I would say, *"I have a thousand generation plan."* That would frustrate those who were sincerely asking, but I had no better response. The Bible says in Exodus 20:5-6:

"You shall not worship them nor serve them; for I, the Lord your God, am a jealous (impassioned) God [demanding what is rightfully and uniquely mine], visiting (avenging) the iniquity (sin, guilt) of the fathers on the children [calling the children to account for the sins of their fathers], to the third and fourth generations of those who hate Me, but showing graciousness and steadfast lovingkindness to thousands [of generations] of those who love Me and keep My commandments."

His Church, His Way

God spoke clearly to my heart. The only way I could plan on a thousand generation degree of influence was to be trans-generational in my thinking and practice and commit myself to being a good spiritual father to sons and daughters who were looking for my example and guidance. I had to think beyond commission to transition.

I was clearly commissioned to both pastoral and apostolic ministry. I realize that there was an accompanying anointing to the call and a supernatural gifting to do what I was called to do. I decided to commit myself both to being planted in the soil of my city, Kelowna, and to growing a spiritual family, Kelowna Christian Center Society.

I had the opportunity to be a stumbling block or a stepping stone for next generational leaders. I was a road maker, but this road was not made to be walked alone. It was not built to be enjoyed privately: it was intended to be a public thoroughfare capable of sustaining a lot of traffic. Another generation had to capture the vision for why that road was built and where that road could take them.

One can count the number of seeds in an apple, but one cannot count the number of apples in one seed. The apple tree that we planted in Kelowna, whose motto is *"Fruitful in Unity,"* has developed an orchard of apple trees, both locally and globally. We have, with good reason, not taken His grace in vain or despised the day of small beginnings.

God promised us, through the Isaiah 61 mandate, that two primary purposes would be fulfilled. We would have a transformational influence on our city of Kelowna: ***"They will rebuild the ancient ruins, they will raise up and restore the former desolations; and they will renew the ruined cities, the desolations (deserted settlements) of many generations"*** (vs 4).

We would also have a transformational influence globally, through sons and daughters: ***"Their offspring will be known among the nations, and their descendants among the peoples. All who see them... will recognize and acknowledge them that they are the people whom the Lord has blessed"*** (vs 9). Whether that was through our schools of ministry, our campus school's Global Citizenship Program, our Building Beyond Borders missional program, or through our online educational influence, that has come to pass.

The task is so large that no individual can accommodate it and fulfill the vision alone. We are one in a chain of leaders called to serve His purposes in this generation. Every one of us is standing on the shoulders of a previous generation, and our shoulders will become the shoulders the next generation will stand on.

- When Moses' time had come, he needed a Joshua: He needed to know who God had in His heart to lead Israel further than He could take them.
- When King Saul disqualified himself from leadership, Samuel needed to recognize who the kingly anointing was coming upon next.
- When Elijah's time had come, and he had a chariot to catch, he needed an Elisha in the wing, someone, who unlike the prophets in training in his day, saw Elijah as a father.
- When Peter rejected his call to the Gentiles, after receiving a heavenly vision, Paul was raised up by God and recognized by the apostolic community to reach the Gentiles with the gospel.

All of us need to be a little more like Joseph who saw way beyond his day. Not only did he fulfill his calling and life purpose, against great odds, he kept his attitude right: *"**You meant it for evil, but God meant it for good**"* (Gen 50:20) and he saw himself as but a part of the plan. *"**By faith Joseph, when he was dying, referred to [the promise of God for] the exodus of the sons of Israel [from Egypt], and gave instructions concerning**"* *[the burial of] his bones [in the land of the promise]*" (Heb 11:22).

Transition requires faithfully speaking into the lives of next generational leaders and preparing them for next steps. Healthy transition occurs when they recognize the metanarrative, when they can see like the Lord, the past, the present, and the things that are to come. They must have this vital DNA ingrained into their mind and heart. True sonship carries the capacity to value highly where they came from (history), to appreciate the cost of what made what they are experiencing possible (present), and to see into what could be (future).

When the Apostle Paul was looking for someone to transition the oversight of the church of Ephesus to, he found Timothy, a spiritual son unlike those around him. This is how he describes it in Philippians 2:19-23:

"I hope in the Lord Jesus to send Timothy to you soon, so that I may also be encouraged by learning news about you. For I have no one else [like him who is] so kindred a spirit who will be genuinely concerned for your [spiritual] welfare. For the others [who deserted me after my arrest] all seek [to advance] their own interests, not those of Jesus Christ. But you know

of Timothy's tested worth and his proven character, that he has served with me to advance the gospel like a son serving with his father."

Paul uses a very interesting phrase to describe the relationship, *"so kindred a spirit."* The term *"kindred spirit"* (or *"like-minded"* in some translations) refers to someone who shares the same mindset, values, and concerns as another person. One may refer to it as *"equally souled."* In other words, if you heard Timothy, you heard Paul: there was no hidden agenda or private ambition to make a name for himself.

It was Paul who encouraged Timothy to think trans-generationally in his leadership: *"The things [the doctrine, the precepts, the admonitions, the sum of my ministry] which you have heard me teach in the presence of many witnesses, entrust [as a treasure] to reliable and faithful men who will also be capable and qualified to teach others"* (2 Tim 2:2). This is referred to broadly as the discipleship hub, the multiplication factor for our faith. However, it also applies to fathers transmitting to sons.

Passing the torch, in a spiritual context, implies the laying on of hands. Laying on of hands is a Biblical process that occasions a transfer of anointing, a divine enduement and an empowerment to help leaders go to next levels. In Elisha's transition, it was referred to as a mantle, and in his situation he received a *"double portion"* that surpassed the ministry of his spiritual father, Elijah.

Transitioning of leadership has never been easy, for either those passing the torch of authority and responsibility or for those receiving it. However, both processes are critically important for the health and success of His ekklesia. One only must think of Christ Himself who on numerous occasions attempted to prepare His disciples for transition.

Even though they had been with Jesus for three years, heard His teaching, been an eyewitness to His moral character and supernatural calling, they all initially failed the test of an orderly transition. We do not see Jesus as the failure here: i.e. a failure to plan, a failure to pick the right people, etc. We do see the challenge that exists within the human heart.

What I do see is the Father's ability to transition authority and responsibility to His Son, who faithfully acted on the Father's will and eternal purpose. What I do see is Christ's capacity to transition authority and responsibility to the Holy Spirit to empower and oversee the emergence of the ekklesia He gave His blood to redeem. What I do see is the Holy Spirit's desire to transition that authority to leaders who carry the heart of the Heavenly Father into the oversight and leadership of His House.

My prayer for years has been: *"Less of me, more of You."* I pray that these principles and values you hear espoused in this book will be a blessing to you. I pray that they will become guardrails on your road of leadership to keep you from going off course. I pray that they will become foundation keys so that you can build according to the Architect's building code.

All of us, like Abraham, are ***"[waiting expectantly and confidently] looking forward to the city which has foundations, [an eternal, heavenly city] whose architect and builder is God"*** (Heb 8:10). I pray that this brings you great joy and hope as you partner in building alongside the One who has promised He would build His Church.

David Kalamen

About The Author

David is the founder of Kelowna Christian Center Society (KCCS) (www.kccsociety.ca) and has led its development for the last forty-two years. KCCS has experienced a profound growth in influence locally, provincially and globally through the numerous and varied ministries it has given birth to.

David is a pastor's kid who lived beside or on top of the church and listened through the vents at the way people talked about God, church and their pastor. What he saw and heard affected his perspective of God, and not unlike a lot of people today, he grew up loving God but not loving the church.

His Church His Way focuses on a new way to

look at government through the example the Father, Son and Holy Spirit have given us. He speaks of seven critical values that form the basis for all healthy function of church government and he addresses seven fundamental cracks in the foundation of modern church structure that need reformation.

By the grace of God, David has lived these values out before his family, leadership and city that he was called to serve. His father, Arnold, along with his son, Brodie and he, have poured over a century of pastoral care into their community.

The Bible makes it clear that we should know those who labor among us, and David, his family and many of the KCCS team, sons and daughters, have decided to grow old together committed to a legacy minded and multi-generational form of leadership.

www.ingramcontent.com/pod-product-compliance
Lightning Source LLC
Chambersburg PA
CBHW061439040426
42450CB00007B/1126